Spreadsheets and prophecy

*An up-close and personal
exploration of the gift of
administration*

Sharon J. Clark

© 2020 Sharon J. Clark

All rights reserved.

Second edition published by UCAN

ISBN: 978-1-5272-9443-1

About the Author

Sharon J. Clark is part of the senior leadership team at New Life Church in Milton Keynes, a multisite church. She leads the Wolverton Mill site and is also the Communications Director for the church as a whole.

From 2010 to 2017 she was employed initially as the office manager, and then as the Operations Manager overseeing a rapidly growing staff team. She became a site leader in 2018, a role that requires strong administrative gifting in addition to many other spiritual gifts. She is passionate about mentoring others in the development administrative skills.

She also serves the Catalyst Network of Churches, which consists of more than 80 UK churches and several hundred churches around the globe.

Her career prior to employment by New Life Church was in the publishing industry. She has always had a passion for the written word, and her poetry and fiction has been published in an array of magazines and anthologies over the years. For more details visit her website: sharonjclark.co.uk

Dedication

To Sue, Hayley and all the many administrators that have
encouraged me, inspired me and supported me.

Contents

Foreword

In 2003 I travelled with a group from my home church to visit churches in Malaysia and Singapore, for learning, mutual encouragement and faith-sharing. When I returned back to the UK, my friends and family wanted to know what would 'stick with me most' from this trip. My answer was simple. I'd travelled halfway across the world to discover during times of prayer, worship and fellowship that it was the same God, the same recognisable Holy Spirit, that was clearly present and at work there. Culturally, the experience was fresh and surprising, but in terms of familiarity, we'd met with members of the same church family and heard from the God we knew and loved.

I had a similar experience when reading this book. Having never met Sharon before, I was hugely encouraged to discover a familiar voice in these pages, championing the Spiritual gift of administration and communicating the same heart for administrators that runs core to UCAN. Simply put, I recognized in Sharon's words, from personal experience and prayer, how God feels about his church and those who serve it in an administrative capacity.

My experience reading this book was a stream of perpetual self-interruptions, having to put down the book to say 'Yes, Yes, Yes!' I hope your experience will be the same. I pray that you will be encouraged, affirmed and challenged as you hear from God, through Sharon, about the interwoven Spiritual gifts of spreadsheets and prophecy...

Andrew Bagwell, Executive Director, UCAN

Preface

Administrators. They are the people who get things done. The often-unseen teams of people who turn vision into reality, setting up and maintaining systems and processes, handling reams of paperwork, and checking projects are compliant with health and safety regulations.

The gift of administration is also the one that is often overlooked. Want a book on prophetic gifting and you will find you are spoilt for choice. Seeking a book on evangelism? There are plenty to choose from. But look for a book on administration, particularly with a focus on it being a spiritual gift, and you will discover slim pickings. This book aims to redress the balance, albeit only in a small way.

Having said that, please be aware this is probably not the book for you if you are seeking a how-to-do administration instruction manual. While it does include some practical tips and guidance on key elements of administration, such as time management, these are skills that can be explored on a wide range of management websites and through secular training opportunities and workshops. This book aims to celebrate administration as a spiritual gift, highlighting the many ways that God blesses the church and moves his kingdom forward through administrators. It will also point to some of the pitfalls that may ensnare us along the way if we are not careful to watch out that our biggest strengths don't also become our biggest weaknesses.

It is a book in which I have attempted to be authentic about life as a church administrator. I am passionate about administration and love to champion all who embrace their gifting in this area. So I invite you to come on a journey with me – to explore the gift of administration and to discover the joy of being called to serve the church with all that you are and all that you were created to be. I hope this book will inspire you, encourage you and even bring healing to you. That is why you will find prayers, questions and even the occasional poem along the way. It isn't a work book, but I pray it is a book for transformation, and that it will touch your heart and reveal something afresh of God's love for you – for who you are and for what you do.

Please note that I have occasionally fictionalised elements of a story, including names, to avoid identification of real-life situations.

Prologue

Genesis 41 verses 25 to 36

Then Joseph said to Pharaoh:

"The dreams of Pharaoh are one; God has revealed to Pharaoh what he is about to do. The seven good cows are seven years, and the seven good ears are seven years; the dreams are one. The seven lean and ugly cows that came up after them are seven years, and the seven empty ears blighted by the east wind are also seven years of famine.

It is as I told Pharaoh; God has shown to Pharaoh what he is about to do. There will come seven years of great plenty throughout all the land of Egypt, but after them there will arise seven years of famine, and all the plenty will be forgotten in the land of Egypt. The famine will consume the land, and the plenty will be unknown in the land by reason of the famine that will follow, for it will be very severe.

And the doubling of Pharaoh's dream means that the thing is fixed by God, and God will shortly bring it about.

Now therefore let Pharaoh select a discerning and wise man, and set him over the land of Egypt. Let Pharaoh proceed to appoint overseers over the land and take one-fifth of the produce of the land of Egypt during the seven plentiful years. And let them gather all the food of these good years that are coming and store up grain under the authority of Pharaoh for food in the cities, and let them keep it. That food shall be a reserve for the land against the seven years of famine that are to occur in the land of Egypt, so that the land may not perish through the famine."

Introduction

Spreadsheets and prophecy – they are not things that people usually consider to be juxtaposed. Surely spreadsheets, with their rows of figures, are the domain of accountants and project managers – a domain that is seen as very down-to-Earth, practical and, let's be honest, rather dull. Prophecy, on the other hand, is a much sought-after gift – part of the spiritual world that is viewed as exciting, creative and inspirational. Run prophetic training in a church and there will be no shortage of people signing up. Offer a class on spreadsheets – well, you know you will probably be safe if you book the smallest meeting room in the building to house it.

However, my personal experience of working in an administrative role for a rapidly growing local church is that the pairing of prophecy and spreadsheets is absolutely essential. Why? Because in all things we should first seek God's vision and direction, and the prophetic gift plays an important role in enabling us to hear his voice. However, once we feel we know where he is leading us, we need to manage the process of reaching the destination that he is directing us to. For that we need the gift of administration, and sooner or later spreadsheets will play a role.

Here I must make a confession. Although this book includes spreadsheets in its title, it is actually about much more than that. The title 'Spreadsheets and prophecy' was dreamt up by Liz Green of Reading Family Church as a seminar title for a leaders' day. All credit to her. She is an excellent example of someone who is a gifted administrator, highly creative and passionate about seeing the advance of the Kingdom of God. Both that seminar, which I delivered with Richard Wightman, lead elder of New Life Church Milton Keynes, and this book were actually about Spirit-led administration. It is about gaining a deeper understanding of the supernatural nature of the administrative gift when it operates in partnership with the Holy Spirit and the full range of gifts that he makes available to us, including, but not limited to, the gift of prophecy.

Let's kick things off by looking at one of the most widely recognised supernaturally gifted administrators in the Bible: Joseph. In particular let's explore the way his administrative gift and prophetic gift intertwined throughout his life.

In Genesis 37 we read that Joseph was the favoured son of his father Jacob, but also it is immediately apparent that God has a plan for his life. He is gifted with prophetic dreams that suggest a future destiny in which he will rise to a much greater level of prominence than his brothers. Poor Joseph – at this point in life his prophetic gift far outweighed his wisdom, and his excited revelation of his dreams to his brothers land him immediately in hot water – sold as a slave, reported as dead to his father, and carried off to Egypt! Clearly, though, there was a calling on Joseph's life – a concept we will look at in Chapter 1 *You are a gift*.

Genesis 39 continues Joseph's story, with verses 2 to 6 giving us our first insight into his administrative capabilities.

> The LORD was with Joseph so that he prospered, and he lived in the house of his Egyptian master. When his master saw that the LORD was with him and that the LORD gave him success in everything he did, Joseph found favour in his eyes and became his attendant. Potiphar put him in charge of his household, and he entrusted to his care everything he owned. From the time he put him in charge of his household and of all that he owned, the LORD blessed the household of the Egyptian because of Joseph. The blessing of the LORD was on

everything Potiphar had, both in the house and in the field. So Potiphar left everything he had in Joseph's care; with Joseph in charge, he did not concern himself with anything except the food he ate.

These must initially have seemed like good years to Joseph. He may even have started to think that this was the fulfilment of his dreams. He was certainly in a place of prominence, much higher than his brothers. However, as his story unfolds we learn that the details of his dreams were significant. At this point his brothers were ignorant of Joseph's rise in prominence. The dreams were only partially fulfilled. Joseph's destiny was entwined with that of a much more important dignitary – the pharaoh of Egypt. But first, his rollercoaster life plummeted him back into prison.

Once again, though, Joseph's administrative gifting brings him into a place of favour. Genesis 39 verses 20 to 23 says this:

> But while Joseph was there in the prison, the LORD was with him; he showed him kindness and granted him favour in the eyes of the prison warden. So the warden put Joseph in charge of all those held in the prison, and he was made responsible for all that was done there. The warden paid no attention to anything under Joseph's care, because the LORD was with Joseph and gave him success in whatever he did.

In the next chapter of Joseph's story – Genesis 40 – dreams come to the fore again. This time, however, Joseph is not the dreamer, instead he uses his prophetic gifting to interpret the dreams of the cupbearer and the baker. It is interesting to ponder how Joseph maintained his relationship with God through all these years of ups and downs so that he could so boldly state in verse 8: "Do not interpretations belong to God? Tell me your dreams." I suspect there may have been many other dreams and interpretations not recorded in Genesis.

Moving on we learn that despite the accuracy of his interpretation and his request for the cupbearer to speak to the pharaoh on his behalf he had to spend two more years in prison before more dreams – this time dreamt by the pharaoh – led to his release. Here, at last, we see his gifts coming together in a really powerful manner.

When he responds to the dreams of the pharaoh he first delivers the prophetic interpretation (Genesis 41 verses 25 to 32). The dreams were a warning that although the land of Egypt would enjoy seven plentiful years, these would be followed by an equally long period of failing harvests and lack of resources. However, he does not stop there, he follows his prophetic insight with some excellent practical advice (Genesis 41 verse 33–36). He recommends that the pharaoh should appoint 'a discerning and wise man' to lead Egypt through both periods, together with a team of overseers in order to store up grain in the good years for use in the lean ones.

Not surprisingly, the pharaoh recognises that Joseph is the 'discerning and wise man' who should lead Egypt through these years. And eventually, Joseph's own dreams are fulfilled when his brothers kneel before him (Genesis 42 verse 6).

Modern-day Josephs

It is true that few of us are likely to be called to lead entire nations through periods of extreme famine. However, if you are reading this book to discover more about using your administrative talents either inside or outside the church, I invite you to open yourself to the expectation that administration and prophetic gifting will be intertwined in your life in a similar manner to that of Joseph. In fact, if you are a Spirit-filled Christian involved in administration I would go as far as to argue that you are called to be a modern-day Joseph, combining prophetic insight with administrative gifts in a supernatural partnership with the Holy Spirit.

It may be that you have never realised that what you do has its source in a supernatural Holy Spirit given gift. In Chapter 1, *You are a gift*, we will explore that truth further. For too long, the gift of administration has been overlooked and even belittled. Now though, just as we have seen other spiritual gifts being restored to the church over recent years, so the value of the gift of administration is being recognised anew.

It may also be that it has never occurred to you that when administration links up with other spiritual gifts it becomes an even more powerful tool in building the kingdom than it is on its own. I honestly believe that the spiritual gifts do not generally work in isolation. Consider for a moment the person you turn to when life takes an unwelcome turn. You go to them because they are wise and will give you good advice but you also go to them because you know that they care about you and will treat you with compassion. Such people are combining the gifts of a teacher or mentor - their wisdom and ability to give you good advice - with that of a pastor – the gift of caring and compassion. So while administration may be your primary gifting, it is extremely unlikely to be the only gift that you have. You may have an evangelistic talent – an infectious enthusiasm that enables you to get others on board with a particular project or vision. Perhaps you are pastoral – the team member others come to when they need reassuring in the midst of organisational change or when they simply need human contact during a task-focused working day. Perhaps you have a teaching gift that enables you to mentor others, bringing out the best in them.

You are almost certainly prophetic! Acts 2 verses 14 to 18 provides a Biblical foundation for the argument that today all Christians have the ability to be prophetic:

> Then Peter stood up with the Eleven, raised his voice and addressed the crowd: "Fellow Jews and all of you who live in Jerusalem, let me explain this to you; listen carefully to what I say. These people are not drunk, as you suppose. It's only nine in the morning! No, this is what was spoken by the prophet Joel: 'In the last days, God says, I will pour out my Spirit on all people. Your sons and daughters will prophesy, your young men will see visions, your old men will dream dreams. Even on my servants, both men and

women, I will pour out my Spirit in those days, and they will prophesy'".

We can all tune into God's voice. Indeed it is God who calls us into his family so I would argue it is impossible to be a Christian without having heard his voice in some way. Now, it is true that not all of us are prophets because a prophet is someone who is recognised as having a high level of prophetic gifting that they use to benefit the church on a large scale. However, as with all the spiritual gifts, the labels reflect the level of gifting and none of us are excluded from employing specific gifts. All of us are prophetic because as Christians Jesus dwells within us and, as 1 Corinthians 2 verse16 tells us: 'We have the mind of Christ'.

For a long time I referred to myself as a prophetic administrator. I saw myself as someone who combined the gift of prophecy with that of administration. Then, one day, a church leader who I consider to have a strong prophetic gift turned my self-given title around and informed me that I was an administrative prophet because my prophetic gifting was actually stronger than my administrative gifting. I certainly didn't object to this re-assignment. I'd never set out to be an administrator and had been somewhat surprised to be asked to take on such a role within the church. In fact I said no to the job at first, but that's a story for another time. The fact was that for most of my life I had worked with words – as an editor and writer. Project management skills had developed alongside the editing and writing through necessity. Editing projects inevitably involve working to a client brief, liaising with other creative people, managing deadlines and, when I worked as a freelancer, all those 'fun' administrative tasks such as invoicing and tax returns. So I didn't really see myself as, first and foremost, an administrator.

But let's not get stuck on labels. The key thing is that we can all bring prophetic gifting to the tasks of administration. And to not do so is rather like having a really great tool in your toolbox but never using it.

Nehemiah's club sandwich

I will come back to Joseph later in this book, but for now let's look at another great Old Testament administrator: Nehemiah. He certainly didn't have the prophetic gifting that Joseph was blessed with but his life was clearly directed by hearing the voice of God. What I particularly like about Nehemiah is the way he positioned the practical elements of administration (the spreadsheet part) between layers of prophetic direction to create a club sandwich model that works as well today as it did in the fifth century BC. Let's take a look at his story.

Nehemiah was the cupbearer to Artaxerxes I of Persia. His story begins when he meets with his brother Hanani who has been spending time in Judah. Hanani informs him that the wall of Jerusalem is broken down and that its gates have been destroyed by fire. Only a remnant of people remain and they are filled with shame at the state of their once-glorious city. Nehemiah is devastated by this news. He weeps and mourns, and begins to pray and fast for the people of Israel. God is using this report from Hanani to speak to Nehemiah about a future in which the walls of Jerusalem are restored. So while we would not label Nehemiah as a prophet – and indeed the book of Nehemiah in the Bible is grouped with the other 'history' books – it is not unreasonable to say that he was moving prophetically in hearing God's voice and prompting to rebuild the walls. Also, as we discover as the story unfolds, that prophetic stirring leads him to call the people of Israel back to their heritage.

Four months pass after Hanani's reporting on the sad state of Jerusalem to his brother, during which time we can assume that Nehemiah was figuring out how he was going to achieve his goal of rebuilding the walls and what he was going to need to do that. Why can we make that assumption? The fact that he is clearly well prepared for the conversation with the king recorded in Nehemiah 2 points to him having used his time in wise preparation. It also seems reasonable to assume that God was allowing him time to work it out because the chapter tells us that

17

he had not been sad in the king's presence until this point – to any outside observer it was business as usual. Now, however, it is time to move things forward and he is afraid when the king observes that he is sad at heart. Having been put on the spot he launches into his request, outlining his vision for the future.

> If it pleases the king and if your servant has found favour in his sight, let him send me to the city of Judah where my ancestors are buried so that I can rebuild it.

> Nehemiah 2 verse 5

However, just as Joseph didn't interpret Pharaoh's dreams and then say nothing more, Nehemiah also goes beyond the God-inspired vision into the realms of administration. He uses his position to access resources – a true spreadsheet moment. Nehemiah 2 verses 7 to 8 records this:

> I also said to him, "If it pleases the king, may I have letters to the governors of Trans-Euphrates, so that they will provide me safe-conduct until I arrive in Judah? And may I have a letter to Asaph, keeper of the royal park, so he will give me timber to make beams for the gates of the citadel by the temple and for the city wall and for the residence I will occupy?" And because the gracious hand of my God was on me, the king granted my requests.

As most of us experience, projects tend to present us with a rollercoaster ride of highs and lows. Nehemiah is no doubt on a high point here because the king has granted his requests. However, he quickly plummets to a low point when he encounters resistance in Jerusalem, as Nehemiah 2 verse 19 reveals:

> But when Sanballat the Horonite, Tobiah the Ammonite official and Geshem the Arab heard about it, they mocked and ridiculed us.

> "What is this you are doing?" they asked. "Are you rebelling against the king?"

Nehemiah refuses to be intimated though. Instead he tosses another layer onto the club sandwich that is sustaining him. This time it is a prophetic declaration recorded in Nehemiah 2 verse 20:

> I answered them by saying, "The God of heaven will give us success. We his servants will start rebuilding, but as for you, you have no share in Jerusalem or any claim or historic right to it."

Prophetic declarations are a powerful tool for us to use when we have heard God's voice but other people or circumstances are attempting to distract us from his direction. More on this later. For now let's finish Nehemiah's story.

In the following chapters we see him using his position to systematically organise the resources he needs for the repairs (Nehemiah 3), and to address further opposition (Nehemiah 4 and 6), Again in Nehemiah 4 (verse 14) he counteracts the opposition by pointing to God.

> After I looked things over, I stood up and said to the nobles, the officials and the rest of the people, "Don't be afraid of them. Remember the Lord, who is great and awesome, and fight for your families, your sons and your daughters, your wives and your homes."

We also see Nehemiah using the gift of discernment when the ridicule turns into sinister plots to discredit him and even to kill him. Nehemiah 6 verses 10 to 15:

> One day I went to the house of Shemaiah son of Delaiah, the son of Mehetabel, who was shut in at his home. He said, "Let us meet in the house of God, inside the temple, and let us close the temple doors, because men are coming to kill you – by night they are coming to kill you."

> But I said, "Should a man like me run away? Or should someone like me go into the temple to save his life? I will not go!" I realised that God had not sent him, but that he had prophesied against me because Tobiah and

Sanballat had hired him. He had been hired to intimidate me so that I would commit a sin by doing this, and then they would give me a bad name to discredit me.

Remember Tobiah and Sanballat, my God, because of what they have done; remember also the prophet Noadiah and how she and the rest of the prophets have been trying to intimidate me. So the wall was completed on the twenty-fifth of Elul, in fifty-two days.

At last the wall is complete and Nehemiah turns his attention to re-establishing community (Nehemiah 7) and worship (Nehemiah 8).

So there we have it – a club sandwich of prophetic direction combined with a strong administrative gift that restored the walls of Jerusalem and drew the people back to their God.

Today we are called to follow in Nehemiah's footsteps – receiving God's vision, making plans to bring it into fruition, refusing to be turned away by opposition, and making full use of prophetic gifts, such as declarations and discernment. We are called to be modern-day Josephs – learning through prophecy what God has planned for the future and using administrative gifts to prepare for the lean years during time of abundance.

Be open to the Holy Spirit

Before you read further, take a few moments to open yourself to hearing the Holy Spirit afresh in your administrative role. Here are some questions that might help you do this.

❐ What is the big picture vision of your organisation? Ask the Holy Spirit to reveal something new to you that will enable you to bring that vision one step closer to reality.

❑ What is the biggest challenge you are facing at the moment? Ask him to reveal the keys of breakthrough to you.

❑ Do you need a fresh revelation of how you fit into the picture? Ask him to reveal the gifts and talents he has given you for this time and place.

The partnership prayer

Holy Spirit, thank you that I am not alone in my administrative role. You are always with me, and I thank you that I can partner with you in all that I do.

I ask now to hear your voice more clearly and to feel your gentle guidance and leading in every situation.

Make me more aware of the supernatural aspects of everyday life.

Help me to combine the supernatural gifts that you have given me so that the sum of the parts is greater than the individual gifts.

Amen

Chapter 1   You are a gift

Kingdom administrators are not Marthas. They are Marys on a mission; worshippers who serve.

(Paul Manwaring, 2014)

Understanding the gift of administration

What is the first thing that springs to your mind when you think about administration? Most of us immediately conjure up images of paperwork, spreadsheets, forms and reports. Perhaps your first thought was 'oh no, the dreaded to-do list'. Your thoughts may have been even less complimentary, perhaps along the lines of: 'It's all that boring stuff that no one wants to do but that has to be done!'

One of the aims of this book is to celebrate administration. Yes, celebrate it! Why? Because administration is a gift, given to us by the Holy Spirit, and as such is worthy of celebration. It naturally follows that administrators – the people to whom the gift is given – are also gifts to the church because they are the willing vessels with whom the Holy Spirit partners.

As someone who spent eight years in church administration and for whom administration is still a vitally important part of my role, I want to shout from the rooftops that administration and administrators are wonderful gifts to the church and the world in general. (Not for my own glory I hasten to add, but for all those hard-working administrators I know who rarely receive acknowledgement for their gifting.) Not only that, I believe that working in administration can, and should, be as much of an adventure with the Holy Spirit as being an evangelist, a preacher, a pastor or a prophet.

So what is the gift of administration? Perhaps the fact that it is often overlooked as a gift is because within churches, particularly those of an evangelical and charismatic nature, the words of Ephesians 4 v 11–12 are particularly well-known and are the often-quoted 'spiritual gifts' verses:

> So Christ himself gave the apostles, the prophets, the evangelists, the pastors and teachers, to equip his people for works of service, so that the body of Christ may be built up.

Leading on from this comes the concept of 'the five-fold ministry', the recognition that for a church to thrive it requires each of these type of people to be actively serving and working in partnership. However, there is another verse, not so frequently quoted, that lists the gift of administration alongside the gifts of miracles, healings and tongues; and the offices of apostles, prophets and teachers: 1 Corinthians 12 verse 28 (ESV).

> And God has appointed in the church first apostles, second prophets, third teachers, then miracles, then gifts of healing, helping, administrating, and various kinds of tongues.

From this it is not unreasonable to conclude that administration is as supernatural in nature as these other ministries, and also as important in the Kingdom of God. After all, on a typical Sunday morning, it is administration that underpins everything, enabling the teacher to teach, the prophets to prophesy, and the evangelists to deliver a life-changing gospel message.

Perhaps another reason the gift of administration is so often overlooked as being supernatural in nature (aside from familiarity with Ephesians 4 compared to 1 Corinthians 12) is that people often think of it as being purely office-based tasks – filing, completing paperwork, sorting out rotas (although turning water into wine may well seem to be a simpler miracle than ensuring all the slots on a rota are filled and the right people turn up at the right time on a Sunday!) These tasks are, of course, important, but administration goes far beyond this, and it is perhaps better to define these as part of the gift of helping – a gift that extends into, and indeed enables, all areas of church life.

Someone who has been highly influential in my life is Paul Manwaring who ran a school of Kingdom Administration that I attended some years back. Paul taught that one of the keys for understanding the gift of administration is to examine the Greek word KUBERNĒSIS, which derives from a verb meaning 'to steer a ship or to guide'. Dr. Larry Perkins, Professor of Biblical Studies, Northwest Baptist Seminary, states that it is this word that is translated as 'administration' in the NIV version of 1 Corinthians 12, and supports Paul's teaching on its definition by highlighting the occurrence of the word in the Old Testament, for example in Ezekiel 27 verse 8, where it refers to the pilot of a ship.

However, the word is also associated with governance and leadership. Perkins argues that the apostle Paul in 1 Corinthians 12 verse 28 uses a plural form KUBERNĒSEIS to refer to acts of direction and governance that provide careful guidance for the church (Perkins, 2012) and therefore the gift of administration referred to here in the English translation is, indeed, much wider than mere clerical tasks. Administrators are called to steer their church or company in the direction identified by its senior leader, who is the person with overall responsibility for setting the vision, whether that is for a church or secular organisation.

OIKONOMIA is another biblical word linked to administration. It is found seven times in the New Testament. Dotan Lesham, who is a historian of economic systems explains that *oikos* is usually translated as 'household'; and 'nemein' is best translated as "management and dispensation" (Lesham, 2016). Combined together the whole word therefore refers to household management. In other words it is about steering a household or family towards a desired outcome or vision. However, Lesham also notes that in Ancient Greece the word was used for the rational management, i.e. administration, of resources in a wide range of other spheres, including law, finance, medicine, architecture, music and military strategy (Lesham, 2016, p. 228).

Finding these particular words in the Bible indicates that God thinks highly of the gift of administration because they are words that carried significant weight within society and referred to people of influence. We can conclude, therefore, that references to administration in the Bible are not focusing on people ticking off check boxes and tasks on a to-do list, but instead they are highlighting a much more active role that involves managing significant resources and processes, and steering people towards a vision. Administrators are the people who map the best way forward, planning, strategising, calculating the risks and creating contingency plans. They manage and steward essential resources; and importantly, they are people who are empowered to make the decisions necessary to achieve success – to arrive safely at a predetermined point in the future. They are leaders who make things happen!

Moses is an outstanding example of someone who had the gift of administration. Here are three ways that he reveals the gift at work. First, in a single night, he organised more than one million people to do the same thing, the same way, at the same time. If you've ever been involved in managing a group of people you will appreciate just how astounding that was! Second, he led the Israelites out of slavery in Egypt and into freedom, with a miraculous crossing of the Red Sea thrown in for good measure. Read through the Book of Numbers to truly grasp the levels of administrative skill needed to marshal and care for such vast numbers of people. Third, he had supernatural encounters with God during which he received the plans for the Tabernacle, and he demonstrated he had the administrative skills necessary to coordinate its construction, including all the internal and external details.

Most of us would be thrilled to have just a small measure of the gift of administration that Moses demonstrated. Whether our own administrative skills are big or small, it is important to understand and remember the purpose of the gift, and to appreciate that it is one of the supernatural gifts God has given to the church. With that foundation administrators can then be correctly recognised as a gift to the church just as surely as an apostle, a teacher, a prophet, a pastor or an evangelist.

❒ Do you understand and fully appreciate the value of the gift of administration? Take a moment to ask God to give you fresh revelation of his view of this valuable gift.

No more 'just'

While we are focusing on the importance of words and their meaning, let's take a moment to look at a small yet emotionally impactful word: 'just'.

If you look up the definition of the word 'just', you will discover it has three excellent uses in the English language. It is a noble adjective that describes something that is based on or behaving according to what is morally right and fair. It can also be used as an adverb to indicate something is good – 'A cup of tea is just what I need right now' – or to give an indication of time – 'Guess what just happened!'

There is, however, a particular use of the word that has sneaked into everyday use and which demeans and belittles people and actions. Worse, all too often, people use it to describe themselves and what they do.

Here's a fictional, but probably all too familiar scenario. Four people meet at a conference and are asked to introduce themselves to one another during a break-out session. Let's take a look at what they say as they take turns to talk about themselves.

"Hi everyone. I'm Jane and I head up my organisation's finance team." She smiles brightly, and nods at the colleague to her left to pick up the baton.

"And I'm Steve," he says. "I'm one of the company project managers with responsibility for our events programme."

The guy next to Steve gives a bit of a shoulder shrug as he speaks. "I'm Ken, and I'm just an administrator."

"Hello. I'm Clare. I just work in the office."

Which of these four people would you immediately consider to have the most important job? You would probably choose Jane. However, a bit more investigation might reveal that Jane works one day a week and her team consists of two volunteer helpers while Clare works full-time and is the vital cog that enables a team of 30 other people to do their jobs well. The word 'just' in these introductions immediately suggested that the work Ken and Clare did was not as significant as that of Jane and Steve.

My experience is that the habitual use of the word 'just' is particularly prevalent amongst those who work behind the scenes in churches. Do you ever hear someone describe themselves as 'just a youth worker' or 'just a prophet'? Absolutely not. Why then do so many administrators tuck this word into their job description? The addition of that tiny little word immediately suggests that administrators and office workers are somehow of less value within an organisation.

For a number of years I ran an annual training event for administrators who are also Christians. As part of the programme there was always a time of prayer and prophecy. One of the key things that the Holy Spirit seemed to regularly address during this time was the hurt and damage caused by people either applying the word 'just' to themselves or having had it applied to them by someone of significance. One of my greatest joys during these days was seeing administrators released from that pain and freely stepping into a full understanding of the truth that they are a gift to the church, an invaluable resource without which much of the church's activity simply wouldn't happen.

Releasing powerballs

This book is titled 'Spreadsheets and prophecy' to highlight that supernatural gifts work together, and that, in my experience, the partnership of administration with prophecy is both natural and essential. As I was writing this chapter, a friend called Sarah contacted me via an online message app. Sarah was the office manager at New Life Church before ill health caused her to give up work. I took on the role and she has supported me in prayer ever since. This is what she wrote:

> I was praying for you last night and God reminded me of a prophetic word Julian Adams gave me the very first time he came to New Life Church, way, way back when I hadn't been working for church all that long.

> I can remember praying and thinking it through over and over because there was something about it that didn't feel as though it fitted quite right. It felt a bit like the correct jigsaw piece that wasn't the right way round to be put in place.

> Over the past 10 years I've returned to it again and again, but have never felt as though it's fitted in quite the way God intended.

> Finally, this week God showed me where it fits. Julian Adams was being rather more prophetic than perhaps he realised. It was the right prophecy, but ten years too early and for the wrong person! His prophecy was:

> "You are more than just an administrator, you are a POWERBALL."

> I'm as certain as I can be that it was meant for you and it was meant for now as you teach and train others and write your book on prophecy and administration.

There was something else that didn't fit quite right with me. God always speaks to me in pictures and as Julian spoke I saw a demolition ball swinging and knocking down an old building. Just like the prophecy, the picture has never completely settled in my heart. A demolition ball is all about destruction and I could only see that as something negative. But now I understand that too. Prophetic administration is a new and powerful way of doing an old job that's no longer a joy, but a chore for many, many administrators. The old buildings need to be knocked down, so that new ones can be built, a bit like new wine in old wine skins. God is ... raising up a new generation of prophetic administrators.

I strongly believe that this word was not meant just for me. Sarah recognised it as being ten years early and delivered to her as the current person in the role, but actually intended for me, the person who picked up the baton from her. I believe I am also a messenger, not the sole recipient, because it is actually intended for all who walk in this role, and so I release it now to you as you read this book.

"You are more than just an administrator, you are a POWERBALL."

☐ Have you ever referred to yourself as 'just an administrator' or as someone who 'just works in the office'?

☐ Has anyone ever described you as 'just an administrator' or spoken of the gift of administration in a manner that demeans its value and what you do?

If you said yes to either of these questions it is time to boot the word 'just' out of your thinking and vocabulary! It is time to start seeing yourself as a gift to your organisation. Reject the lie that you are 'just an administrator' and declare the truth that you are a gift to the church. If someone has described you in this way or made you feel that the gift of administration is somehow a lesser gift than forgive them for doing that. Forgive them for the way it made you feel. Declare the truth of who and what you are.

Here's a prayer of declaration to help you.

The powerball prayer

Father God,

I thank you for the gift of administration.

I reject the lie that my skills and abilities are of lesser value than those of other people.

In the name of Jesus, I forgive those <insert names if they come to mind> who have made me feel otherwise.

I declare the truth that I am a gift to the church because of who I am and what I can do. I declare that I am a powerball called to build new things to the glory of your name. I declare that I am an administrator with a supernatural gift, working in partnership with the Holy Spirit, and that I can achieve far more than I can possibly dream or imagine with you.

I hold fast to the truth of Ephesians 2 verse 10: I am God's handiwork, created in Christ Jesus to do good works, which God prepared in advance for me to do.

Amen

Recognise your calling

> Now Moses was tending the flock of Jethro his father-in-law, the priest of Midian, and he led the flock to the far side of the wilderness and came to Horeb, the mountain of God. There the angel of the LORD appeared to him in flames of fire from within a bush. Moses saw that though the bush was on fire it did not burn up. So Moses thought, "I will go over and see this strange sight – why the bush does not burn up."
>
> When the LORD saw that he had gone over to look, God called to him from within the bush, "Moses! Moses!" And Moses said, "Here I am."

> Exodus 3 verses 1 to 4

Recognising your calling is one of the keys to accepting that you are a gift to not only the church but also to your wider community.

However, when Christians start to talk about recognising a spiritual calling the conversation can all too quickly soar into the stratosphere, opening the door to an expectation of supernatural encounters. The story of Moses and the burning bush in Exodus 3 can sometimes be held up as the benchmark experience for being called into the destiny that God has prepared for us. And indeed, for some that will be their experience, but dare I suggest that for the vast majority of us the journey towards recognising our spiritual calling is much less dramatic and clear cut. Even some of our modern-day Christian role models did not discover their calling through burning bush experiences.

Let's explore the story of William Wilberforce as an example.

William Wilberforce – changing the face of a nation

Wilberforce is often held up as an example of a man who had a clear calling from God to bring about the abolition of the slave trade in Britain in the 1800s. Scratch the surface of his life, though, and we find that recognising this calling was not a straightforward affair.

He was born in Hull in 1759 and inherited a fortune at the age of 9 when his father died. This money enabled him to do whatever he wished to do. As a young man he studied at Cambridge University but also indulged his love of fine dining, wine and gambling. Aged just 21 he became the youngest member of the House of Commons when he spent more than £8,000 (equivalent to almost half a million pounds today) on fighting and winning the general election battle for Hull in 1780. However, his motivation at this time was far from selfless. He openly admitted that his key aim was his own distinction and that he 'did nothing – nothing of any purpose' in his first years as a member of parliament (Piper, 2006, p. 10).

The first indication that God had a higher plan for Wilberforce can be traced to 1784 when he invited Isaac Milner to join him on a holiday in France. Milner had been his house master at school before becoming a tutor at Cambridge, and the two men were good friends. Wilberforce was surprised to discover that although Milner had become an evangelical Christian he did not display any of the stereotypical negativities that had become associated with such a faith at this time in history. The two men reportedly talked for hours about Christianity. At the same time Wilberforce stumbled over a book entitled '*The Rise and Progress of Religion in the Soul*' by Philip Doddridge. Milner described it as one of the best books ever written, and by the time Wilberforce finished reading it in February 1785, he described himself as having reached an 'intellectual assent to the biblical view of man, God and Christ' (Piper, 2006, p. 29).

In November 1785 Wilberforce had 'an intense spiritual experience, making him feel that his own past life was futile, that he was utterly dependent on the infinite love of Christ, and that his future life must be committed to the service of God' (Wolfe, 2004, p. 55). He described this encounter with God as his conversion experience and it radically changed his life, moving his understanding of the Christian faith from an intellectual exercise to a life-changing experience. However, he did not know how to translate this new state of being into a practical outworking. His close friend, the Prime Minister William Pitt, tried to persuade him to steer clear of evangelical Christianity, warning him it would make his talents completely useless. It would certainly do him no favours as evangelical Christians were the subject of much mockery and scorn at this time (an experience we can perhaps empathise with today).

Finally, in desperation, Wilberforce turned to a family friend from his childhood days, John Newton, an Anglican priest who is best known as the writer of the hymn Amazing Grace. Wilberforce's key question was whether he could serve both God and parliament. Should he withdraw from politics and take up a role in the church? Newton's response was to have a profound impact on the future of not only Wilberforce but also the nation. He replied, 'God has raised you up for the good of the church and the good of the nation, maintain your friendship with Pitt, continue in Parliament, who knows that but for such a time as this God has brought you into public life and has a purpose for you.' (BBC website, 2011).

The rest, as they say, is history. In a journal entry in 1787 he wrote about his sense of calling saying that 'God Almighty has set before me two great objects, the suppression of the Slave Trade and the Reformation of Manners [moral values]'. He remained in politics and was instrumental in bringing about the abolition of slavery in Britain, and was also the author of a best-selling book that challenged the practice of paying lip service to Christianity and championed Christian beliefs as the foundation of a better society.

So with Wilberforce we see a young man who clearly had an encounter with God that radically changed his life. The discovery of his spiritual calling, however, involved the counsel of friends as well as his own sense of what God was setting before him. It was Newton who recognised Wilberforce as being a gift to both the church and the nation, and encouraged him to take full advantage of the circumstances into which God had placed him. Subsequently, Wilberforce's calling involved him recognising the things that he was good at – his ability to speak in public, his skill with words, and a natural charm that enabled him to persuade people to his cause. He also put more tangible gifts to good use, particularly the wealth he had inherited.

What can we learn from Wilberforce, bearing in mind he was a politician not an administrator? The answer is that, when trying to identify a spiritual calling, a good starting point is to ask yourself what you are good at. Our natural gifting comes from God, and he has created each of us with a unique purpose, and so the gifts and skills we have are a good indication of the things he is likely to call us into.

Finding your niche

Because you are reading this book, it is reasonable to assume you are good at administration in some form. The next question regarding calling, therefore, is about situation. In what circumstances should you be using your gifting? Are you called to be an administrator within a church setting or should you be using your gift in the secular world? Perhaps you will have seasons of operating in one area and then in the other. It is certainly not unusual for God to use the secular world as a training ground for a heavenly purpose.

Think again of Moses. He was born into humble and dangerous circumstances – the Israelites were an enslaved minority in Egypt at this time and their infant males were the subject of a death warrant issued by the pharaoh (Exodus 1). However, his mother's attempt to save his life by placing him in a waterproof basket on the Nile led to him being found and adopted by an Egyptian princess. Raised in the royal palace he would have received the best education available and also have experienced first-hand the administrative and political workings of a powerful nation. This early training must have been invaluable when he later found himself leading and feeding thousands of people through the desert.

Few of us will face a challenge of that order of magnitude (thankfully!) What is important, however, is for all of us to use our talents for the things that God sets before us in whatever arena we find doors that are open.

Let's take a look at Daniel as an example of someone who applied himself to the opportunities God opened to him.

Daniel – called to influence in Babylon

Daniel is a fascinating character because, in addition to being a significant prophet, he was also an important governmental servant in Babylon who utilised the gift of administration to great effect. And on top of all that he was an excellent historian, faithfully recording God's dealings with him.

The first chapter of Daniel explains how he was called, prepared and blessed of God, and also provides a concise record of the historical setting for the whole book. Daniel 1 verses 1 to 6 says this:

> In the third year of the reign of Jehoiakim king of Judah, Nebuchadnezzar king of Babylon came to Jerusalem and besieged it. And the Lord delivered Jehoiakim king of Judah into his hand, along with some of the articles from the temple of God. These he carried off to the temple of his god in Babylonia and put them in the treasure house of his god.

> Then the king ordered Ashpenaz, chief of his court officials, to bring into the king's service some of the Israelites from the royal family and the nobility - young men without any physical defect, handsome, showing aptitude for every kind of learning, well informed, quick to understand, and qualified to serve in the king's palace. He was to teach them the language and literature of the

Babylonians. The king assigned them a daily amount of food and wine from the king's table. They were to be trained for three years, and after that they were to enter the king's service.

Among those who were chosen were some from Judah: Daniel, Hananiah, Mishael and Azariah.

Clearly, therefore, Daniel was a smart young man of noble background. It is interesting to speculate what his future might have been had Jerusalem not fallen into the hands of Nebuchadnezzar. What is certain is that he would not have imagined spending most of his life as a captive in Babylon. Once there, however, he and his three companions made the most of the intellectual opportunities that were laid before them. Leapfrogging over the story of their request to eat vegetables and drink water rather than the rich food and wine of the royal palace, Daniel 1 verses 17 to 20 describes how God blessed them, and Daniel in particular, and they entered into the King's service.

To these four young men God gave knowledge and understanding of all kinds of literature and learning. And Daniel could understand visions and dreams of all kinds.

At the end of the time set by the king to bring them into his service, the chief official presented them to Nebuchadnezzar. The king talked with them, and he found none equal to Daniel, Hananiah, Mishael and Azariah; so they entered the king's service. In every matter of wisdom and understanding about which the king questioned them, he found them ten times better than all the magicians and enchanters in his whole kingdom.

The story continues in Chapter 2 with Daniel not only interpreting the King's dream but first he and his companions having to overcome the challenge of discerning what the dream was, something that had defeated all of the Babylonian astrologers and wise men. Verses 48 and 49 describe the response of a grateful Nebuchadnezzar:

Then the king placed Daniel in a high position and lavished many gifts on him. He made him ruler over the entire province of Babylon and placed him in charge of all its wise men. Moreover, at Daniel's request the king appointed Shadrach, Meshach and Abednego administrators over the province of Babylon, while Daniel himself remained at the royal court.

And so we have, in a story not without similarities to that of Joseph, an Israelite with the prophetic gift of dream interpretation being raised up to high office in a foreign land, and entrusted with the administration of vast resources and land. But whereas we know that Joseph had an expectation of his calling to higher things through his own dreams, there is no indication that Daniel had any foreknowledge of his future nor that he spent time puzzling over his calling as many of us do today. He simply set himself to rise to the challenges before him to the best of his abilities.

Listen for your calling

So to summarise – a calling can be loud or soft. Some people have an equivalent experience to Moses hearing his name called from a burning bush. For others a call will come through prophetic dreams or words. But sometimes, as in the case of William Wilberforce, it is simply knowing that what you are doing is the right thing for you.

And let's not forget – however we recognise the call – we are a gift to those around us. Without administrators nothing gets done. The most wonderful and world-changing ideas have precious little value until someone takes the first step of turning a dream into a reality. And the moment that step is taken the gift of administration comes into play.

☐ Are you aware of a clear calling on your life? If so, what do you need to do to be obedient to it?

❐ If there is no clear calling, what opportunities are opening up before you? In which workplace areas can you serve God through your administrative skills, whether in the secular arena or within the church?

Hold on tight

To close this chapter on knowing that you are gift, let's briefly look at the importance of holding on tight to that truth.

Have you ever taken a moment to admire the tenacity of those who achieve their God-given vision? Think of Joseph who, as a youth, had a dream that one day people would bow before him, but then lived through years of unfulfilled expectation during which his life didn't just get entrenched in the treacle of stagnation, it plunged him to the lowest of places as a prisoner in an Egyptian jail – falsely accused, forgotten by those he aided, and apparently abandoned by God. Yet through it all he held onto his faith and kept believing there was a brighter future ahead. Then there is Nehemiah, who faced the plotting of those around him to not just put an end to his vision for the walls of Jerusalem, but to bring about his death. He steadfastly focused on the task God had laid before him, refusing to be distracted and therefore entrapped by the plans of his enemies.

A few years back my husband and I took a small team to the Philippines to support the work of a charity we had been involved with for some time. The charity had been birthed from a vision to see street children lifted out of poverty and given a hope for the future. Over the years it had grown steadily and achieved a great deal and was now being run by one of the founders' daughters – a young woman had gone to the Philippines for a short-term trip when she was 16, and had never returned, making it her home. Married to a Filipino she had two children of her own, plus three Filipino children that she and her husband had saved from the streets and were in the process of officially adopting. The charity was positively impacting the lives of hundreds of children and families.

I was aware that she had been through difficult times in the previous 12 months. One evening she took me up onto the roof of the unfinished building that was home to a dozen children who had previously lived on the streets to tell me of the plans for the upper storey. As we stood in the warm evening sun, amongst bags of cement, bricks and a small concrete mixer she began to share some of the difficulties she had lived through. The key word underpinning it all was 'betrayal'. Her heart was broken. She was emotionally exhausted.

I can't remember exactly what I said in reply, but I do know that it was something along the lines of pointing out all that she and her husband had achieved over the years. Somewhere along the way I know I reminded her of the calling on her life. Her experience of discovering her calling was a Wilberforce-style journey of applying her skills and gifting to the things that God had set before her. To paraphrase Newton's words, God had raised her up to be a gift to the nation of the Philippines. Finally I prayed with her and encouraged her to continue on.

Many months later, possibly even years when my husband and I returned to the Philippines with another team, she told me that our conversation on the roof had been deeply significant. She had been on the verge of giving up, and was seriously thinking of packing up and returning to the UK with her family. Instead she realised that the Philippines was her home, and the work of the charity was her mission in life. No doubt there were other factors – and other God moments – that enabled her to find the strength and the courage that she needed to continue but a key part was being reminded of her calling and an encouragement to hold fast to that.

Since that time the work that she and her husband have achieved through the charity has grown in significance. She is now a woman with an influential voice in the city, and I am sure God has greater things yet to reveal for her.

We all face difficult times in life. Indeed, Chapter 7 in this book is entitled *When it all goes wrong* and tells of a time in my life where the challenges seemed overwhelming. For now, though, let's focus on the simple truth that we all need ways to find the strength and courage to press on when it feels like we are in the middle of a storm, with no end in sight. We need to be ready for when the enemy does his best to convince us that we have no value or sends people we trust to derail us from our mission – think of William Wilberforce being told by his best friend that becoming a Christian would do him no favours.

I have a picture of a heron in my office because it is a reminder of the calling I had to leave the job I loved in the secular world and instead work for the church. On the days that I wonder if it is all worthwhile, I look at that picture and remind myself that I am doing what I do because God raised me up for such a time as this (again borrowing words from Newton). It reminds me that I am a gift to the church even if I feel anything but gift-like.

I also have a picture of a lion on my office wall because that reminds me that I am not alone in the tasks and challenges I am facing. Rather it is God who is building His kingdom and I have the enormous privilege of being along for the ride. This picture also reminds me of the lyrics of the song Lion and the Lamb by Brian Johnson and Amy Renée – a great worship song for lifting the spirits!

Our God is the Lion, the Lion of Judah
He's roaring with power and fighting our battles

He's coming on the clouds, kings and kingdoms will bow down
And every chain will break, as broken hearts declare His praise
Who can stop the Lord Almighty?

(Mooring, Brown and Johnson, 2014)

So, hold on tight to your calling and the knowledge that you are a gift from God to those around you. Find ways to regularly remind yourself of these things – whether that is through an object or keeping a record of prophetic words over your life or ensuring you have good friends around who will encourage you when you are weary, uphold you in prayer and bring joy to your life in the midst of a storm. And do remember, you are a powerball!

❏ What tools do you have in place to restore your strength when weary?

❏ How can you keep focused on the truth that God has raised you up for such a time as this when circumstances would tempt you to throw in the towel?

A prayer for times of stormy weather

Father God,

Thank you that I am called to serve you to the best of my ability in all the things that you set before me.

I accept the truth that you have raised me up for the good of the church and the good of my community. I declare the truth that you have a purpose for me and I was born for such a time as this.

Give me the strength and courage to remain focused on you and to know who I am in you – a beloved child to whom you have given gifts and talents to partner with you in releasing Heaven on Earth.

When I feel weak, I ask that I will remember that my strength comes from you. Guide me through the storms, and enable me to continue on until I have achieved all that you have ordained for me.

I thank you that you are the Lion of Judah. That I can trust you to fight my battles for me, and that no one can stop you!

Thank you Father that you go before me and you walk beside me.

Amen

References

BBC (2011) 'William Wilberforce' [online]. Religions: BBC. Available at: http://www.bbc.co.uk/religion/religions/christianity/people/williamwilberforce_1.shtml Accessed 13 June 2018.

Lesham, D. (2016) 'Retrospectives: What did the Ancient Greeks mean by Oikonomia?', *Journal of Economic Perspectives*, vol. 30, no. 1, pp. 225–231.

Manwaring, P. (2014) 'The importance of administration', Blog post, available online at: http://www.paulmanwaring.com/posts/the-importance-of-administration. Accessed 8 August 2018.

Mooring, L., Brown, B. and Johnson, B. (2014) 'The Lion and the Lamb', *Have It All,* Bethel Music.

Perkins, L. (2012) 'The Gift of "Governance" (KUBERNĒSIS) (1 Corinthians 12:28)', Blog post, available online at: http://moments.nbseminary.com/archives/122-the-gift-of-governance-kubernesis-1-corinthians-1228/. Accessed 14 September 2019.

Piper, J. (2006) *Amazing Grace in the Life of William Wilberforce*, Crossway Books, Illinois, USA.

Wolfe, J. (2004) 'William Wilberforce', in A207 From Enlightenment to Romaticism, c.1780–1830: Block 3 Religion, Exploration and Slavery, Open University, Milton Keynes.

Chapter 2 What is your why?

*Don't underestimate the power of your vision to change the world.
Whether that world is your office, your community, an industry or a
global movement, you need to have a core belief that what you
contribute can fundamentally change the paradigm or way of thinking
about problems.*

(Doctor Leroy Hood, Healthcare pioneer)

The birth of a vision

The past four days had been hugely inspiring, and now they were
drawing to a close. I had been unbelievably blessed by the
teaching of Paul Manwaring who had set up and led a School of
Kingdom Administration at Bethel Church, Redding. I was
grateful to him and his team for all he had taught, and in
particular for making me realise that administration is a gift from
the Holy Spirit: that it is a supernatural gift, and that I had a
calling in this area. I was also grateful to the other students of
administration for making me realise I wasn't alone. There were
many like-minded people out there and it was possible to be part
of a mutually supportive network of administrators. I must also
add that I was grateful to my church, particularly Richard
Wightman, for enabling me to attend the school. It was no small
deal to take a week out of work and fly to the United States for
teaching on administration.

As I prepared to fly home a vision caught hold of me. But before I go into detail on that, let me give some background on how I ended up in a meeting room in Redding with about twenty other administrators from around the world.

In January I had left a job I loved – one that came with the best financial package of my career – and I had stepped into the complete unknown of working full-time for New Life Church in Milton Keynes. Until this point I had spent most of my working life as a writer and editor. There were some project management skills needed for that, particularly for the freelance business that I ran alongside an employed staff position. The job also involved some interaction with people, especially clients whose needs I aimed to understand and deliver on. Most of my time, though, was spent crafting words into, hopefully, various forms of high-quality communication. The beauty of words, I realised with hindsight, is that they generally go where you put them, do what you ask of them, and they never argue or answer back.

My new role involved managing people, mainly volunteers, and reviewing and upgrading administrative processes in a small, but soon-to-be fast growing church office. I quickly discovered that the team of volunteers I inherited, all of whom were lovely people to chat with over a cup of tea, were not necessarily enthusiastic about change. On top of this there was an undercurrent in the environment that made me feel administration wasn't valued in the same way as, say, pastoral skills. While all the other teams in the church were described as 'ministries', what went on in the office was described as 'support services'.

I knew I'd been called into the role – both by Richard, who, I was later told, had rather determinedly head-hunted me, and also by God. I did try to say no to both of them, but discovered them to be equally tenacious in their pursuit of me – however, that is a story for another chapter. A few weeks into the job, with the office beginning to run more efficiently and the church growing steadily, I was painfully aware that I was running things based on my personal experience rather than with any specific training or, indeed, vision for the future. I knew my number one priority was assisting Richard in moving forward with the vision he and the eldership team had for the church – a vision that I strongly believed was God-given – but there was a part of me that wanted more. I wanted to build on a strong Biblical foundation, a Spirit-led foundation, rather than the patchwork quilt of my experience, made up as it was of past failures and successes.

It was then that I became aware of the Bethel School of Kingdom Administration – four days of teaching and encounter led by Paul Manwaring. I put in a request to attend. Richard agreed to the proposal. And off I went, with no real idea of what to expect. It was an eye-opening time, and much of what you will find in this book stems from those four days. Although I knew I had been called to work for the church in the area of administration I didn't really understand what that entailed. Now, though, I saw what the gift of administration was and had a fresh appreciation of its purpose. I came to realise that I didn't have to do things alone, but rather I could pair this gift with my prophetic gifting in partnership with the Holy Spirit. For the first time since taking on the role I was truly excited about it. It was like all the pieces of a jigsaw puzzle suddenly fitted together and I could see the big picture. And like most people who have a major revelation I wanted to tell everyone about it. That's the moment in which a vision for the future was birthed.

As I packed up my pens and notebook for the final time at the school, I knew I wanted to share what I had learnt with folks back in the UK. I was painfully aware that few UK administrators had the freedom to do what I had just done. Attending the school in Redding was an expensive undertaking. There was the cost of a transatlantic return airfare, a further return flight from San Francisco to Redding, and then four days of food and accommodation to pay for. On top of the financial expense there was the challenge of carving out the time in a busy diary. Although I didn't have a particularly large network of administrative friends at the time, I was aware that I was fairly unique in being a full-time member of staff with a boss who was willing to let me disappear for a week, as well as an extremely supportive husband who could and would juggle our family life around his own full-time employment.

The vision I had that day was for Paul Manwaring to deliver his four-day school in the UK. Right then and there the likelihood of that happening seemed an impossibility. Bethel church was big on working through relationship with people, something we didn't have with them at this time. And Paul, although British by birth, seemed well settled in the USA where he was part of the senior leadership team at Bethel.

However, to cut a long story short, seven years later I had the enormous privilege of introducing Paul to a group of approximately 30 UK church administrators at the start of a four-day training event in Milton Keynes, England.

It was a demonstration of a key truth: when God gives us a vision, he also sets in motion the events to bring it to fruition.

As administrators it is important for us to understand the importance of vision both in our working lives and on a personal level. As Chapter 1, *You are a gift* explains, administrators are the people who steer things in a given direction to enable a vision to become a reality. We therefore need to know what vision we are working towards, and to fully understand how that vision can be outworked in practice. On a personal level, we need a vision that is applicable to the season of life in which we find ourselves. A personal vision encapsulates 'your why'. It is the reason you get out of bed on a cold winter's morning. It is the reason you press through when times are tough. It is the reason you find joy in simply being you.

While this book does not attempt to be a manual on 'how to be an administrator', this chapter does contain some practical advice on understanding and setting vision, mission, strategy and objectives. If you are an administrator in a church, some of this may seem to be an overly corporate approach. However, businesses and churches that are seeking to grow will share much in common from an organisational viewpoint. The key difference is that those working within churches can partner with the Holy Spirit in shaping things for success – spreadsheets and prophecy truly link together. Although, of course, if you dig into the corporate world you will find there are more than a few highly successful businesses around that have been pioneered by Christian business people who, no doubt, also partner with the Holy Spirit. The gift of administration is not just for the church. Likewise, proven business tools are not just for the corporate world.

What is your vision?

Vision is vital. It is impossible to emphasise this too much. As Proverbs 29 verse 18 tells us: 'Without vision, the people perish'. Other translations use different words, some referring to 'prophetic vision' and some saying that people 'cast off restraint' or 'run wild'. Whichever translation you favour the underlying message remains the same: vision is vital.

It is also vitally important not just to have a vision statement that is written on paper and then rarely considered, but rather for it to be the foundation stone on which everything you do rests. Let's talk about collective vision first.

In a recent workshop, I asked a group of church leaders and administrators if their church had a vision and, if so, could they tell me what it was. Most of them confidently said that yes, their church had a vision statement. However, hardly anyone in the room could voice it aloud with confidence.

To be honest, I wasn't surprised by that. At New Life Church, we had recently gone back to the drawing board on our vision when we realised that not even our elders could readily recite it. What value was a vision statement that was overly complicated and, even if it was remembered, immediately raised further questions as to what it actually meant?

So what did we learn at that time?

First, that a vision statement should encapsulate where we are going as a church. It should communicate our aspirational goal. In essence, it should be a prophetic statement that captures a picture of the future.

Here are just three examples of good vision statements from the charity sector and business world:

- World Vision – For every child, life in all its fullness

- Disney – To make people happy

- Google - To provide access to the world's information in one click.

If you want more examples you can Google them easily enough – simply type 'vision statement examples' into the Google search box. And there you have proof of the success of Google in turning their vision into a reality. They are so good at what they do their company name has become a verb synonymous with searching the internet.

Here's a quick quiz for you:

☐ Do you know what the vision is for your church or company?

☐ Can you readily recite your vision statement?

☐ Does your vision statement underpin everything you do?

If you answered yes to these questions, congratulations! Feel free to skip the next section. However, if the answer is no, then it is time to look afresh at your collective vision.

Now, you may be in a role where you can easily bring that about. However, if the opposite is true and you don't feel you have any influence over the setting of a vision statement, be brave. Raise the issue with those who do. Gently point out that to do your job well, it is important for you to work towards a vision that is communicated well. Most people understand it is far easier to steer towards a well-defined landmark than a vague destination.

So how do you create a memorable vision statement?

At New Life we realised our existing vision was far too long, and that it was in fact three different statements that read more like an instruction manual than a prophetic goal. No wonder we couldn't remember it. Seeking advice we discovered that the recommended maximum length for a vision statement is just eleven words. Eleven! Ours was at least forty. You can see from the three examples in the previous section that two of the vision statements are barely half that number of words. Google flops a toe over the line with one extra word, proof that as with most things there are no hard and fast rules, but rather an underlying principle. In this case the important thing is to keep it short.

❏ How many words are in your current vision statement? If there are more than eleven consider a serious edit.

Next came the difficult step of trying to figure out what we wanted our vision to be. Our eldership has a great mix of the five-fold gifts listed in Ephesians 4 verse 11. Richard, who leads the church, is both apostolic and an excellent strategist. Also around the table we have elders and senior team members who are strongly gifted in the areas of teaching, worship, pastoral, evangelism and prophecy. Everyone had an opinion on our vision, and not surprisingly a lot of those opinions were coloured by the particular gifts of the people concerned. Our evangelist strongly argued for an outward-focused vision. Our pastoral leader emphasised the need for the vision to be caring and loving. It quickly became apparent that writing a vision by committee was not going to work.

Things began to move forward when the views and prophetic insight of the elders and our senior team were handed over to a trio of people who are gifted communicators. They were tasked with crafting a short inspirational prophetic statement that was both evangelistic and pastoral. How hard could that be?

I don't recall exactly how long we worked on this, but it was at least six months, with different versions of the statement being discussed, revised and rejected at our monthly elders meetings. It was painful. At times it was hugely frustrating – it is surprising how much time can be spent on discussing the merits of one word compared to another. It forced us to constantly seek God's direction. But it was vitally important that we got this right and didn't settle for something that was merely good enough. So where did we end up? Our vision is:

To be a community that loves God and loves people.

Does it work? Well, we have been operating under this for about three years now and yes, it does. First, it ticks the boxes of being short and easy to remember (ten words - hurrah!). Communicating it to our church family was a vital first step in making it our foundation stone, so we plastered it everywhere we could think of putting it: on the home page of our website, on our printed literature, on our rolling Sunday morning slides, on our social media. We worked it into sermons and it is the first thing we talk about with newcomers who are interested in making New Life their home church. People absorb it often without even realising where they have come across it.

It is also works as a checkpoint for new activities. Whenever something fresh is proposed, our vision turns into a question. Does this activity help us to be a community that loves God and loves people? If yes, we will consider it in more detail. If no, then it goes no further. It is a really useful and absolutely essential tool for keeping us focused.

The wording is also broad enough that it met with the approval of both our pastoral and evangelistic champions. The pastoral team can interpret loving people in terms of caring for their needs – physical, emotional, spiritual – while the evangelists interpret loving people as telling them the gospel and enabling those who don't have a relationship with God to encounter his love.

It also works as a good foundation on which to build a mission statement. However, before moving onto collective mission, let's take a look at the importance of having a personal vision.

What is your personal vision?

As administrators it is important to know where we fit in the jigsaw puzzle of the big picture of a collective vision. Most administrators are great at focusing on what needs to be done. It is a key part of our gift set. However, merely 'doing things' will quickly grow tedious if we aren't caught up in a bigger picture, namely the sense of purpose that gets us out of bed in the morning to drive through traffic and foul weather to our desks. It is the answer to the question: what is your vision for your role and for yourself? Or, in other words, what is your why?

I distinctly remember the day that I caught something of my personal vision for the future. It was 2011, and I was at a conference in Brighton that, up to this point, had been an annual event for leaders of newfrontiers churches. This year was different though. It was the final conference of its type because Terry Virgo, the founding father of newfrontiers, was handing on the leadership to the next generation.

Terry is a modern-day apostle who, in the late 1970s, had a strong calling from God to build something new in the UK and beyond. With Terry handing things on, Nigel Ring, an outstanding administrator who had worked alongside Terry from the beginning, turning vision into reality, was retiring from his administrative role. As Nigel was honoured and celebrated on stage one evening I caught a glimpse of how he had served Terry over the years and I knew that I wanted to serve Richard in that way. By this point I had been working full-time for the church for more than a year, but I was totally focused on the stuff that needed doing. Now I saw things differently – now it was about partnership, not tasks.

My memory is hazy from those days. I do remember talking about this with Richard on the drive home. I certainly didn't spend time crafting a short but inspirational vision statement for myself. However, looking back I realise that I mentally formed one and, indeed, spoke it out on occasions. It was simply this: to make Richard's work life as easy as possible so he could focus on the big picture strategy rather than on the day-to-day running of the church.

It is important to remember that on a personal level we can have a big picture vision for our lives – perhaps something along the lines of: to serve God with all my heart, with all my mind, with all my energy – but also a more defined personal vision that serves the season we are in. Having a personal vision for our lives does not mean we have a step-by-step plan for the years ahead, but rather we know what journey we are on and welcome the fact we are constantly moving forward.

I am writing this at a time when I have recently handed on a number of responsibilities and in their place taken on a new role as a site leader within the church. As a result I have had to think afresh about my personal vision for the next few years. Our staff team has grown to a point where Richard has an executive assistant, we now have a finance team rather than a single book keeper, and we have developed a very different structure of operation with a senior staff team that is currently five strong but likely to increase over time. Having said that, serving the vision of New Life Church and Richard as its senior leader will always underpin the things that I do.

I am also at the stage of life where my husband is planning to retire within the next couple of years. We are looking forward to there being considerably more free time in his diary and figuring out how that enables a long-held joint vision to engage in more overseas mission.

There are lots of websites that provide advice on identifying and shaping your personal vision. Nearly all of them agree that taking the time to do this is valuable. Without it we run the risk of drifting aimlessly through life and arriving at a place of disappointment because the life we are living is not the life we dreamed about when we were younger.

So if you don't know what your personal vision is, how do you set about finding it? The key starting point is that you need to know yourself. Vision comes from your hopes and dreams and is influenced by the intrinsic values that you live by. Here are some questions to help you figure it out.

❏ What are your most deeply held values?

Take some time to work out the values that you live by. Think about the people and experiences in your early life that had the greatest impact on you. Think about what was happening during these experiences. What was going on and what values were you honouring in that situation?

Think about times when you have been frustrated and angry. What values were being suppressed in those experiences?

What things are essential to you for your mental well-being? Perhaps you love to learn new things or to have a creative outlet.

To help you reflect on this, here are the core values we identified for New Life Church: authentic, accepting, courageous, honouring, generous, team-based.

It is important to know and understand your values because they define who you are, and they influence what you do and the decisions you make.

❏ What motivates you?

Take the time to work out what really matters to you. Ask yourself 'What do I want to do?' If you come up with things you feel you 'should' do set those to one side for now. For this exercise focus on things you 'want' to do, and for each one you ask yourself why that is. This will help you to uncover what really motivates you. Bear in mind that motivation can be both extrinsic, for example, something done for external reward such as a good salary, and intrinsic, something done because it simply brings you pleasure. You may wish to spend some time considering how you balance these two types of motivation in your life.

❐ What do you desire in life?

As Christians we are often wary of talking about our desires, but when we are looking to identify our personal vision it is important that we focus on the things we want to attain, rather than on things we want to get away from. Think about where you want to go in life, not the things you would prefer to leave behind.

❐ Do you dare to dream?

Ask yourself questions such as: what would I do if I had unlimited resources? Don't limit yourself to the things that you think are possible in the here and now. Remember that a vision encapsulates a prophetic statement of the future. Be creative. Be playful. Allow yourself to dream. Jeremiah 29:11 (NIV) states this:

> "For I know the plans I have for you," declares the LORD, "plans to prosper you and not to harm you, plans to give you hope and a future".

❐ Is your personal vision in alignment with God's will?

Be led by the Holy Spirit as you ponder these questions. He is the one who has given us our gifts and talents. He releases dreams to us. Partner with him, and see where he leads you. It is important to know that we are working in partnership with him on the plans that he has for us because it enables us to push through the tough times.

Be aware also that God provides us with freedom to choose. Just as we wouldn't insist that a child of ours followed a particular path that we picked out for them, my experience is that God rarely dictates a narrow future to us. Often when I pray with people about their future direction I will see a prophetic picture of many doors, all of which lead to good places. He is a good father, not a controlling dictator.

One more thing to bear in mind regarding personal vision is to avoid the trap of believing that opposition means you have misheard God's voice. Nehemiah used prophetic declarations to press on when he faced opposition. In Nehemiah 2 verse 20 he sets his face against the ridicule of Sanballat the Horonite, Tobiah the Ammonite official and Geshem the Arab who are mocking him and attempting to divert him from his vision to rebuild the walls of Jerusalem. Instead of being downcast by his situation he declares this:

> "The God of heaven will give us success. We his servants will start rebuilding, but as for you, you have no share in Jerusalem or any claim or historic right to it."

He knew that he was working on plans revealed to him by God. He was not going to be diverted by a lack of popularity and some verbal abuse. When we know that our personal vision is in alignment with God's will, we can rest assured that he has our backs and will be with us no matter what.

With time, prayer and thought you will hopefully arrive at a point where you can now answer this final question with confidence:

❒ What is your personal vision for your current season?

Once we reach that point we can then get intentional about making it happen.

Out of vision comes mission

Often people use the terms 'mission' and 'vision' as though they are interchangeable. However, these two concepts should be quite different from each other. In the context of this book – and I think generally in business – mission is an amplification of a vision. It answers the questions of what a vision looks like in practice. What does it involve?

We looked at three vision statements earlier. Let's now compare them to their company's mission statements.

World Vision

Vision statement: For every child, life in all its fullness

Mission statement: World Vision is an international partnership of Christians whose mission is to follow our Lord and Saviour Jesus Christ in working with the poor and oppressed to promote human transformation, seek justice and bear witness to the good news of the Kingdom of God.

Disney

Vision statement - To make people happy

Mission statement: The Walt Disney Company's objective is to be one of the world's leading producers and providers of entertainment and information, using its portfolio of brands to differentiate its content, services and consumer products.

Google

Vision statement: To provide access to the world's information in one click.

Mission statement: To organise the world's information and make it universally accessible and useful.

As you can see, while the vision statements of these companies are aspirational, their mission statements begin to look at the details of what is needed to reach their goal.

For us at New Life Church we developed a three-sentence mission statement that widened each of the key words in our vision. Recall our vision is to be a community that loves God and loves people. Now here is our mission statement:

> Community is being family together, and all are welcome. We love God and take every opportunity to encourage everyone to encounter him and experience His love for themselves. We love people too, and do everything we can to encourage them to be all God created them to be.

In developing this we asked lots of questions beginning with W. What do we want community to look like and to be like? What are the ways in which we can practically express our love for God? Naturally we would want others to experience him and to discover how amazing his love is. What does it look like to love people? That was perhaps the trickiest one as loving people can take a myriad of forms.

After yet more deliberation, we felt we'd eventually arrived at wording that was missional in nature, yet facilitated different interpretations by people with different spiritual gifting. Again, both our evangelists and our pastoral team were content with the wording because they could read it through the lens of their gifting and see the mission within.

❑ What is your mission statement?

❑ How closely does it reflect your vision statement?

❑ Does it provide pointers for what is needed to turn vision into reality?

Know the plans I have for you

So, having crafted the words for both vision and mission what comes next? This was the point where we rolled up our sleeves and started thinking much more short-term and much more in the practical realm. It was time to create a strategy for the next year or two.

At this stage, and with that timescale in mind, we were still looking at big picture goals. We asked each of our department leaders to come up with one key objective for their area, and to make it a SMART one. SMART objectives are widely used in the business world. The acronym is not always defined in the same way, but here is a common definition, and the one that we adopted.

S - specific

M - measurable

A - agreed upon

R - realistic

T - time-bound

As with our work on the vision and mission we spent time praying and seeking God for his direction.

There is always a danger when making plans that we come up with lots of great ideas for things we could do as a church. After all there is no shortage of needs to meet. In our city we are aware that homelessness is a big issue. We also know that people are lonely. One in four children live in poverty (a shocking statistic given the apparent wealth of the city). Many people are living with crippling debts. The mental health of people of all ages is a big concern. We could come up with all sorts of project ideas and initiatives for these issues and more besides. But what is God calling us to do in this next season?

As in all things, it is vital to align ourselves with His plans. As Jeremiah 29 verse 11 makes clear, his plans will prosper us and give us hope. Prophecy comes before spreadsheets – or in this case, before strategic objectives.

Also, it is important to recognise the value of putting time and effort into only one or two objectives over a realistic time frame for delivery, perhaps six months or a year. Being focused encourages success.

Writing this has made me realise that we should probably review our objectives at the next elders' meeting as strategy is a key item on the agenda. It is all too easy to spend a lot of time and effort in creating objectives and strategies and then to simply put them in a drawer and forget about them. Instead, we get drawn into reacting to the latest and seemingly urgent issues that crop up in day-to-day life. It is important to stay focused on the big picture.

❏ What is God saying to you about the future?

❏ Based on that, what are your strategic goals for the next one or two years?

Making collective strategy personal

If you've worked in a large organisation, you may well have come across the concept of team objectives. These are often big picture goals handed down by a distant management team and chances are you may simply roll your eyes and ask what they have to do with you. I have to confess that has been my experience, and I know others who have been frustrated by team objectives over which they feel they have no personal influence nor any way to contribute to their achievement. Needless to say this is not a good scenario for anyone. The ideal is for everyone, at all levels of an organisation, to understand how their specific role fits into the picture, and therefore why it is of value.

At New Life we therefore have another level of objectives that sits under our big picture strategy. These are the annual objectives set for each department by the department leader, and the objectives for each person within a department set by that person in discussion with the leader. The department objectives are written in a simple table in a Word document with the first column containing the why. For example the why for our Sunday morning hosting team is 'To make everyone feel valued and welcomed on arrival'. There is a clear link between this and our vision to be a community that loves people. In the second column there is a set of bullet points that outline how we are going to achieve that. The third column lists who is going to do what. Finally there is a column for information on budget items.

When we first introduced this system it seemed like a lot of unnecessary work, but now we value the fact that it is a vital final step for defining priorities for the year and keeping us focused on the things that we believe are achievable and valuable.

Part of the process is also regular reviews, with a half-yearly review being particularly valuable for identifying what has been achieved to date and what still needs to be done.

Alongside the work-related objectives, we also have written personal development plans. These cover a wide range of things from reading Christian books to improving personal fitness to honing creative and spiritual gifts. We encourage people to include the things that energise them, and also to keep a check on work-life balance. The words of Jesus recorded in John 10 verse 10 are this:

> The thief comes only to steal and kill and destroy. I came that they may have life and have it abundantly.

It is important for our well-being that we experience life in all its abundance, and that we avoid the siren call of overly long working hours and the resultant impact on friendship, family and fun.

So, to close this chapter on What is your why? here is one final question:

☐ What do you do for no other reason than it is fun?

As you ponder all of this, admittedly rather process-driven stuff, this prayer may be helpful.

The abundant life prayer

Father God,

Thank you for all you have given us and for the lives that we lead.

Take us deeper into you. Show us where to walk that we might walk with you.

May we always remember that you have plans to prosper us and to give us hope.

Help us to embrace who we are, and to know and understand the values that we live by and the vision to which we are called. Help us to know our why.

Let us see that some destinations can be reached by different paths. Sometimes there is no right or wrong path, just a choice of scenery. May we not forget that you walk those paths us. We are never alone and never without your guidance and your love.

Thank you for giving us an abundant life. Help us to receive and enjoy that abundance.

Amen

What is your why?

What is your why?
Your reason for being.
The driving force that makes it worthwhile
To get out of bed
on a cold, storm-filled morning.

What is your why?
Your purpose for living.
The solution you bring to the world that you touch
Uniquely gifted to you
by your history.

What is your why?
Your unique selling point.
The viewpoint you bring that colours the world
With a shade from infinity
that is yours alone.

What is your why?
The difference you'll make.
Whether large-scale or small, whether noticed or not
Without which the world
Will be a much poorer place.

Chapter 3 The gift of time

People assume that time is a strict progression of cause to effect, but actually, from a nonlinear, non-subjective viewpoint, it's more like a big ball of wibbly-wobbly, timey-wimey ... stuff.

(Dr Who, 2007)

God of the elastic time

I am a huge fan of science fiction, and so tend to adopt phrases from my favourite shows. The title of this chapter comes from Doctor Who. In a 2007 episode called Blink, the tenth doctor, played superbly by David Tennant, provides the excellent definition of time given above. Because we experience time in a linear fashion, it is easy to assume that is its nature, but delve into the topic online and you will quickly discover lots of scientific debate on the subject, including arguments that time is just an illusion and that it doesn't actually exist. I have to confess such articles fascinate me, although I quickly get lost in the details. And I do love the – possibly fanciful - idea that time can be wibbly-wobbly. One thing I am sure about, however, is that God is not constrained by the bounds of time – real or illusionary. And one of the things I've learnt as an administrator is that sometimes he will make time stretch so we can do far more in an hour or a day than we thought possible.

We know God has many names. Perhaps the most familiar is Jehovah Jireh, meaning God will provide. Other names are Jehovah Shammah: God is present, and El-Shaddai: God

Almighty. I have a personal name for him – God of the elastic time.

I remember the day I had four important things to do, one of which was to transcribe a number of prophetic words for a meeting the next day. If you've ever transcribed spoken words you will appreciate it is a process that does not lend itself to short-cuts. It is necessary to listen to every word on a recording in order to produce an accurate transcription – even if the aim is to capture the gist of the recording in text form rather than a word-for-word report. My best estimate on this occasion was that the task would take me an entire morning, if not longer.

However, much to my astonishment I found myself completing the task within a couple of hours. Now some of that was down to very practical reasons – recordings that were relatively easy to condense and transcribe for example. And it is possible, of course, that I misjudged how much time I would need for the task. However, I was bemused by the speed with which the task had been completed. I was only too happy to give praise to the God of elastic time who makes all things possible.

If this all sounds too far-fetched take a moment to read part of the story of Hezekiah in 2 Kings 20 verses 8 to 11. The chapter opens with the king falling ill and being told by Isaiah to put his affairs in order because the illness would prove fatal. In response he tearfully appeals to God, who then tells Isaiah to deliver a different message – that Hezekiah will be healed and will receive a further fifteen years of life. On the third day from this new message he will be recovered enough to go to the temple. Perhaps it is not surprising that Hezekiah found this sudden turnaround difficult to accept, even though it was good news. On hearing it he asks for a sign.

> Hezekiah had asked Isaiah, "What will be the sign that the
> LORD will heal me and that I will go up to the temple of
> the LORD on the third day from now?"

Isaiah answered, "This is the LORD's sign to you that the LORD will do what he has promised: Shall the shadow go forward ten steps, or shall it go back ten steps?"

"It is a simple matter for the shadow to go forward ten steps," said Hezekiah. "Rather, have it go back ten steps."

Then the prophet Isaiah called on the LORD, and the LORD made the shadow go back the ten steps it had gone down on the stairway of Ahaz.

What does it mean for the shadow to go back ten steps? The astonishing answer is that God reversed time as a sign that His promise to heal Hezekiah was true! He is the God of elastic time!

Not enough hours in the day?

I will return to the wibbly-wobbly nature of time later, but for now let me share a memory of watching an episode of Stargate SG-1 called Thor's Chariot a few years ago. This was another favourite TV show of mine, involving a team of interplanetary explorers who faced dangers and life-threatening experiences on a weekly basis. After one particular adventure, during which the team had narrowly escaped with their lives, Daniel Jackson, the team's archaeologist, observed that they would need to hole up for a while until things calmed down. In response, Teal'c, a warrior from another world, drily commented, 'Things will not calm down, Daniel Jackson. They will in fact calm up.'

I laughed at the humour, but deep down the sentiment resonated with me. I was forever hoping that things would calm down, but it certainly seemed that the contrary was the norm. Life just got busier and busier. I stopped saying that I needed more hours in my day and upped my complaint to the more dramatic cry that what I really needed were more days in my week. Somehow the list of things to do always seemed to far exceed the amount of time available to do them.

Something needed to change, and since it was unlikely that my to-do list would shrink in size, what I needed was time management. But not just a human-resourced time management programme, rather I needed a Spirit-led time management system.

But before delving further into that here is a different, yet pertinent question. Should being overly busy be our everyday experience of life?

I don't believe it should be. In fact, I suspect the enemy is rather pleased with himself if he can keep us flat out busy with stuff, constantly ruled by the next pressing deadline, instead of taking time to rest and to simply be in God's presence.

A Biblical view of time management

We may think that time management is a modern concept but there are some great Bible verses that fit the theme. Take a look at 2 Corinthians 9 verse 8 for example:

> And God is able to make all grace abound to you, so that having all sufficiency in all things at all times, you may abound in every good work.'

What a great verse. God provides for all our needs, including giving us the time that we need for 'every good work'. Clearly Paul also understood that God is outside of time and space, and worthy of the name God of the elastic time.

There are also warnings to make good use of time. The writer of the book of Hebrews chastises the Christians in Jerusalem for not making the best use of time when he writes in Chapter 5 verse 12:

> By this time you ought to be teachers, you need someone to teach you again the basic principles of the oracles of God. You need milk, not solid food.

He is unimpressed that they haven't been wise stewards of their time, frittering it away instead of using it to grow in the grace and knowledge of God.

Paul writes in a similar vein in Colossians chapter 4 verse 5, saying:

> Walk in wisdom toward outsiders, making the best use of the time.

Perhaps his encouragement to make the very 'best use of the time' was fired up by the truth written in Proverbs 27 verse 1 that none of us know what comes tomorrow or whether tomorrow will even come since we "*do not know what a day may bring*", and the somewhat amplified version of the warning in James 4 verse 14 that we:

> ... do not even know what will happen tomorrow. What is your life? You are a mist that appears for a little while and then vanishes.

So how can we go about living in the truth of that instead of arriving at the end of the working day with a sense of frustration because there is still so much not yet done? Or worse, a sense of panic that things won't get done in time and the world will somehow come crashing down on us.

I'd like to say that I have this topic cracked and now glide through life as serene as can be. The truth is that I am often like a swan, apparently calm and unruffled to the shore-side observer, but paddling like mad beneath the surface. Here though are some tips – the things that I remind myself of when the panic is rising, when I find myself waking in the night mentally checking through my to-do list, and when I just need things to calm down.

Holy Spirit prioritisation

There are lots of great time management tools available, but none of them beat asking the Holy Spirit to guide you. Ephesians 2 v 10 tells us that we are 'created in Christ Jesus to do good works, which God prepared in advance for us to do'. So, if he has prepared things in advance let's ask him what his plan is for the day. When I remember to do this, I do find my days go so much smoother then when I don't. To be honest I don't know why I don't do it every day knowing that it is true, but there you go, I'm not always particularly smart. I only tend to remember to consult him when I'm faced with half a dozen urgent things that all need to be done yesterday.

Sometimes it is only in hindsight that I realise the Holy Spirit was nudging me in a certain direction. Today was one of those occasions. I decided 'on a whim' to head into town to post a package to a friend in Australia. It is a task I have needed to do for several days now, but I'd been prevaricating. However, as I finished my morning's work, there was the package sitting neglected on the sofa in my study. It was time to act.

I headed into town, walked to the Post Office and sent it off. On the way back down the High Street, I remembered I needed some more shower gel so I popped into our local branch of Boots. It is a relatively small branch with a pharmacy and only two staff on duty, neither of whom were in view. There was quite a long queue at the pharmacy counter as I took my purchase to the general service counter. From my vantage point I could see the two staff members were busy behind the scenes, presumably serving people with prescriptions for medication.

An elderly lady joined me, holding a packet of paracetamol and some plasters. After a couple of minutes she asked if anyone was serving, and I nodded towards the back.

'There are two staff, but they seem rather busy. Hopefully they'll be back in a moment.'

She glanced at her watch. 'I hope so. I have an appointment to get to.'

The minutes ticked by. A third lady joined us with a basket of goods. She also looked at her watch, and muttered about needing to get to the school to collect her children. The elderly lady grew more agitated as still no one came to serve us. One of the two staff appeared with items for the person at the front of the pharmacy queue.

The elderly lady set her items down on the counter, shook her head and said she couldn't wait any longer. She headed for the door. Seconds later the other staff member appeared, handed medicines over to someone else in the pharmacy queue and then came to serve me. The lady with the basket, turned to call the elderly lady back, but it was too late she was already at the door. We looked at each other and then at her discarded items.

'What if I paid for her items and ran after her,' the lady with the basket said, voicing the idea that had already formed in my head.

'I'll pay,' I immediately responded. My bank card was already in my hand. 'You do the running.' I looked at the person now manning the till and pointed to the pills and plasters. 'Ring these two things up first.'

As soon as she scanned them, the lady with the basket grabbed them and ran out of the shop, while my own items were scanned. She returned moments later, somewhat breathless but with a big smile.

'I caught her up. She was really pleased. So grateful.'

Now I was grinning too. 'Great team work,' I said.

'Well,' said the person behind the till. 'That's something I don't see every day!'

I had no idea when I headed out of the house 'on a whim' that the Holy Spirit was setting up an opportunity to demonstrate generosity and to bless an elderly lady in a hurry. He has prepared good works in advance for us to do.

Tips for time management

Time management, in keeping with the theme of this book, is another area where we can combine spiritual gifting with natural gifts and tools. The prophetic aspect of time management is found in seeking the Holy Spirit's direction for the day. The natural comes in the form of the many excellent time management tools available to us. Search the web and you will be presented with more than 27 million results. Here are just a few practical suggestions to consider when seeking to improve your time management skills.

The master to-do list

We are huge fans of lists at New Life Church. The more complicated our processes and plans have become, the more we have realised that lists are essential. As an administrator, a master to-do list will be a very good friend. The sooner you can figure out what format of list works for you the better.

Some people adore software tools that create lists for them. Personally I prefer a much simpler approach. My master to-do list is a four-column table in a Word document that sits on the desktop of my laptop. The column headings are: Area; What; Further detail; By when.

'Area' is the big picture label for a task. At the moment I have topics such as 'Ministry team' and 'GDPR' listed as well as various special Sunday services, e.g. Father's Day.

'What' covers the key activity I need to complete, e.g. create a plan, etc. 'Further detail' then contains a list of smaller actions to achieve that goal. Finally, and importantly, 'By when' is the completion date I need to (or want to) hit.

The advantages of this simple way of working are the ease with which things can be added or removed, and also the speed with which I can scan the 'By when' column and therefore prioritise my time. The 'By when' column also helps to inform my request for guidance from the Holy Spirit, which often takes the form of a prayer asking which of a number of urgent items is the most urgent in his view.

One key thing with a to-do list is to bear in mind that it is there to serve you, not the other way around. I don't use it as an exhaustive list of everything that needs doing in a week. Some routine tasks are just that – so routine I don't need to put them on a list to know I need to do them. Some quick and easy tasks get put right at the top of the first page above the table because they are just there to jolt my memory and don't need to be fleshed out in detail. And sometimes I colour code items – green if I've actioned something part-way but am now waiting on someone else to do something before I can progress it further. I sometimes colour things red if a deadline is approaching, usually larger items that require a block of time to complete.

❐ Do you have a to-do list system that works for you? If not, experiment with various options until you find one you like.

The weekly or daily to-do-list

Once you have a master to-do list operating well for you, the next step is to use it to create either weekly or daily lists, perhaps both. On Mondays I have a batch of routine tasks that need to be done for the week – the ones I don't bother to put on a to-do list because they are habitual – and if I don't do them someone in my team will be nudging me on Tuesday in order to do their part of the process. Most Mondays I also handwrite a list of six or seven items that need tackling that week. These get prioritised by urgency, the amount of time needed to complete them, and also whether or not they are things I enjoy doing.

I'm a lark. I am most productive in the mornings. So I know that is the time to tackle the tasks that need me to be smart and awake. I also try to tackle the things that I don't really fancy doing because I am way more likely to grit my teeth and plough through something that is important but not energising before lunch than after. In the early afternoon I can happily tackle tasks that require a bit of creativity. By 4pm my best use of time is answering emails that need a response but no strategic thought.

You may be the opposite, doing your most focused work in the afternoon or even later. I know of one person who comes alive at 11pm and will happily work through to 3am. Each to their own – I also know not to expect coherent conversation with this person before 10am in the morning.

The key is to know yourself, and where possible develop routines that work for you.

❐ Are you a lark or an owl? Schedule tasks to suit your body clock where possible.

The email battle

Email – love it or hate it, we all have to deal with it. One of the most useful pieces of advice another administrator gave me was to point out that – like a to-do list – email is a tool that should serve me, not the other way round. It is tempting to log in to email at the start of the day and then leave the programme running so email alerts are constantly popping into view. I don't know about you, but I can't resist the temptation of looking to see what an email is about if I recognise the name of the sender (which is most of the time).

Most days now I try to limit checking email to the start and end of the day. There are then three ways to deal with them:

1. Delete the junk.

2. Respond (which might be as simple as forwarding the email to another team member for action).

3. Transfer requests and actions in an email to my to-do list (copy and paste wherever practicable).

I've learnt the hard way not to allow my email inbox to become another to-do list. For one thing I found myself wasting huge amounts of time reading emails more than once or scanning up and down my inbox looking for things. Secondly, it is way more efficient to have everything that needs to be done in one place. My ultimate aim is to have an empty inbox at the end of each day. To be honest that is a rare occurrence. However, I can usually get it down to less than a dozen, which personally I find gives me peace of mind.

☐ Is your email inbox dominating your life? What processes can you introduce to take back control?

Using your time wisely

"What is important is seldom urgent and what is urgent is seldom important."

(Attributed: Dwight D. Eisenhower, 1954)

Do you ever have days where you feel you spend all your time reacting to things rather than proactively dealing with the urgent stuff on your to-do list. A useful tool for guarding against your time getting sucked up by tasks that really ought to be at the bottom of the list is the urgent–important matrix. If you've read Stephen Covey's book *The Seven Habits of Highly Effective People* (Covey, 1989) you may already be familiar with this. It is interesting to note that there is some debate regarding the origin of the matrix, with it often being attributed to the US president Dwight D. Eisenhower. It is often referred to as the Eisenhower Matrix.

Whatever name you use, the matrix is a great tool for prioritising tasks because it asks two key questions:

1. Is this task important?

2. Is this task urgent?

Once you have the answers to these questions you can put each task in the relevant quadrant of the matrix (see the diagram below).

Urgent and important	Not urgent but important
Urgent but not important	Neither urgent nor important

Let's look at each of these quadrants in more detail.

Quadrant 1: Urgent and important

This quadrant is for the highest priority tasks that are best tackled straight away. It is the 'now' quadrant (see the next diagram).

Ideally there should relatively few tasks located here. If there are lots then it suggests you have taken on the role of a troubleshooter and finding time to work on longer term plans will be difficult. If you are constantly troubleshooting it will probably be worth taking time out to investigate your organisation's processes, and to look for the reasons behind tasks regularly becoming both urgent and important. Are you understaffed for example? Or perhaps a lack of delegation to others is the root cause? Eisenhower was reported to be a master of delegation when it came to tasks and authority (Neely, 2017). The only thing he did not delegate was policy setting.

If two or more tasks appear to be equally urgent, then you may need to dig a little deeper, perhaps talk to the people who are waiting on you to complete these tasks so you can prioritise which is the most urgent. Within church life, I have also discovered that only a few people have a grasp of the big picture priorities, but they are surprisingly flexible once the priorities are explained to them. For example, a small group leader may ask for your help with a task they consider to be vitally important but that you know is not going to be viewed with the same level of urgency within the church office. People are surprisingly adapt at finding alternative solutions to their task-related problems when they realise they will have to wait a while for the office team to get to it.

Managing the expectations of other people is actually a key part of getting the urgent and important stuff done. When I first started managing the church office the prevailing culture was to deal with the request of anyone who happened to drop in. In particular the photocopier was considered to be available for anyone to use (donations welcome). This would perhaps have been fine if people knew how to use the photocopier and didn't require support. As the church grew rapidly in size it quickly became apparent we needed to shift the culture so we didn't lose large chunks of the day assisting people with their personal printing needs. These days people know to make appointments with office staff and drop-ins tend to only be for emergency pastoral issues (which are few and far between).

Quadrant 2: Not urgent but important

This quadrant is the place for the tasks you should spend most of your time progressing. It is the 'later' quadrant.

The tasks allocated here are important but not urgent, so there is time to do things well – rather than desperately trying to hit a deadline. This means there is the opportunity to produce high-quality work in an efficient manner.

Surprisingly, however, these tasks are often the ones we tend to neglect. The key to avoiding that is to plan time for them in your diary so you can work on them free from interruptions and also so they don't get pushed out by other tasks.

The kind of tasks that sit in this quadrant are the strategic planning ones that enable you to set goals for the future and to shape things to fit with your vision and mission. Don't forget, this includes weeding out things that might be perfectly good ideas and plans but that draw resources and energy away from your agreed vision.

Quadrant 3: Urgent but not important

Danger lurks in this quadrant so try to have very few tasks allocated here. Why is it considered a dangerous place? This is because urgent but not important tasks can cause you to be very busy but not in the least bit productive. Most often these tasks originate with others who 'need your help' – remember the photocopier available to all church members. To counteract this danger try to think of it as the 'delegate' quadrant where you get others to do as many of the tasks as possible.

Most administrators want to be helpful – serving others is a key part of the role. However, it is important to not simply say 'yes' whenever urgent but not important tasks arise. Instead it is more helpful to manage people's expectations and, if you can, direct them to another way of achieving what they need to do. These days most of our events are managed with online sign up. We appreciate that not everyone is confident with using the internet, or indeed has access to it, however, wherever possible we encourage people to find a church friend who can assist them rather than asking the office staff and volunteers to help. That not only provides them with the tech support they need, it also helps to build community and allows others to feel of value.

Something else to watch for in this quadrant are tasks that exist simply because 'we've always done it this way'. As a team we are trying to ask 'why' much more.

Why, for example, is the refreshment team still arriving an hour before the meeting starts if the new coffee machines brew in fifteen minutes? (Turns out there are other things to do that still require the early start.)

Why are we running a particular event? We've recently reduced our church family meetings from two a year to one a year because we have grown too large to operate in consultation with the entire church family and there are often better ways to communicate information than gathering people to a special meeting.

Our new mantra is 'always start with the why', especially for things that have been done before.

Quadrant 4: Not urgent and not important

It can be fun to do things in this quadrant but to be effective we should ideally avoid spending much time here because this is the zone for trivial tasks. For me, these are end of the day tasks when my brain is tired but I still want to do something useful. For example, I might schedule two or three Facebook posts – fun, a bit creative, and it ticks my box of building community.

The danger of this quadrant is that a quick ten minutes can morph into an hour or more – especially if social media is involved. So as with all things, if we can find the discipline to schedule things, all the better. Having said that, we all need more relaxation in the working day and there is nothing wrong with rewarding ourselves with a fun, non-urgent, not important task once we've made good progress on other stuff.

Having worked through the quadrants let's add a bit more information to help with time management.

Urgent and important	Not urgent but important
The now zone	The later zone
Keep to a minimum	Spend most time here
Urgent but not important	Neither urgent nor important
The delegate zone	The trivial zone
Beware the danger of being busy but not productive	Be highly selective about tasks

Will your time management be easy and resolutely efficient if you employ this matrix? Probably not, but it is a good tool to bear in mind. I use it to colour code my to do list – red is urgent and important, amber is a mix of quadrants 2 and 3, everything else is in black type, which means it will get looked at eventually (or it will get bumped into colour).

References

Dr Who, Season 3, Episode 10, Blink, BBC 1. First aired 9 June 2007.

Covey, S. R. (1989) *The Seven Habits of Highly Effective People*, Simon and Schuster, UK edition 2005.

Neely, J. (2017) 'How to increase your productivity with the Eisenhower Matrix', Blog post. Available online at: https://blog.toggl.com/eisenhower-matrix/. Accessed 24 July 2019.

Chapter 4 There is always enough

And God is able to bless you abundantly, so that in all things at all times, having all that you need, you will abound in every good work.

(2 Corinthians 9 v 8, NIV)

An extravagant surprise

On a very ordinary Thursday afternoon, working my way through a long and complicated guest list for an overseas conference, the ringing of my phone was more annoyance than welcome distraction. As is often the case, the call was about a somewhat random topic. Someone in the church had spotted the appeal for Christmas shoe boxes for children in need in the Philippines, and noted that canned fish was one of the items listed for inclusion. He had access to a stock of canned fish – would the charity be interested in it?

'How many cans are we talking about?' I asked.

'Quite a lot', he replied.

'Are we talking tens of tins?'

'More like hundreds,' he answered.

'OK, I'll ask and let you know'.

I hung up, sent a Facebook message to my contact at the charity, who was, indeed, interested, and then put them in touch with each other. I didn't think any more about it until a week later.

My mobile alerted me to a message from my charity contact. It said this:

> 'Just wanted to let you know that we picked up the first load of cans from your contact. We are coming back for the rest next week. In total there was 4,700 tins of fish and 4 tonnes of pasta! This means we have enough for all our extra shoe boxes, the buckets of love project we run each Christmas, and for a children's home we now work with in the north of the Philippines. We cannot thank you enough.'

I stared at the message in disbelief, then in total amazement at what God can do. A random phone call and a quick Facebook message had led to this. I laughed with sheer joy at the abundant favour of the one who owns 'the cattle on a thousand hills' (Psalm 50 verse 10). With God there is always enough – and often there is far more than we can ever imagine.

Several months later I visited the Philippines, and found myself sitting around a table with a team of staff and volunteers from the charity. Freshly cooked tuna was a popular choice on the menu, and as it was served one of the volunteers turned to me and began to tell me the story of the 'Christmas of everlasting tuna'.

'We were so blessed,' she said. 'There was so much tuna we were able to use money from the budget that had been set aside for food to buy other things.' She then described in detail all the ways that life had been improved because of the tuna donation. I found myself laughing with joy once more. God in his infinite kindness wanted me to know there had been yet another chapter to the story. His blessing continued on and on. He really can, and frequently does, do far more than we could ever imagine possible.

Changing the way we think

In John Chapter 6 we can read the story of Jesus feeding a crowd of 5,000 hungry people who had gathered to hear him teach. We are told that Jesus decided to use the situation to test Philip. In verse 5 he poses a question to Philip: 'Where shall we buy bread for these people to eat?' Philip doesn't answer the question but instead, in verse 7, immediately points out the lack of resource saying: "It would take more than half a year's wages to buy enough bread for each one to have a bite!"

One of the biggest challenges facing anyone involved in church administration – and actually in church life in general – is overcoming the temptation to believe that the problems and issues we are facing are far larger than the resources available to us. If we look only at our circumstances we can quickly point at areas of current lack: finances, people resources, and that frequent complaint of administrators, lack of time.

However, if we turn a current lack of resource into a belief that this is the way things will always be then we will buy into the enemy's desire for us to believe that God is not a generous father who has unlimited resources – resources that he is willing and able to make available to us.

I recently attended a two-day training event designed to help us recognise the things that are a bottleneck to growth in our current situation. The event kicked off with a really inspiring talk by Craig Groeschel, the founder and senior pastor of Life Church, the largest church in the United States of America. At the time of writing it had 27 locations in eight states. Craig began his talk by telling us to change what we think is possible. His argument was simple. If we don't believe that something is possible, we will prove that it is not.

Believing that something is possible is much more powerful than simply engaging the power of positive thinking. It is an action that enables us to look at what God can do and to rely and trust in him, rather than looking at what we can humanly achieve and relying and trusting in our own strength. Ephesians 3 verses 20 and 21 say this:

> Now to him who is able to do far more abundantly than all that we ask or think, according to the power at work within us, to him be glory in the church and in Christ Jesus throughout all generations, forever and ever. Amen.

This is such an exciting verse. God can do far more than we can imagine. When we start living life with the belief that we aren't even fettered by our capacity to think of something, we suddenly realise that there are no limits in God. Feeding 5000 is certainly not a challenge to him.

New Life Church went multisite in September 2017. Our thinking six months later had expanded to the possibility of a third site and a church plant into a nearby town. But, if I am honest, a lot of my thinking had been about what we can't do rather than what we can. I was hugely challenged by Craig, who talked about running six services in a week at certain locations, and told us that not only was this possible, he and his team had been challenged by a younger leader to run eight. Their initial reaction of that being impossible had been overturned when this leader demonstrated the opposite. Eight services a week! That certainly expands my thinking on what can be done.

So the first step towards living a life in which there is always enough is to change our thinking.

❏ In what areas is your thinking about what is possible limited?

We have a generous father

I recently returned from a walking holiday in Scotland. When I was preparing for the trip I made a mental note to buy an elastic hairband. My hair isn't particularly long and I never tie it back in my daily life, but when walking in the wilds of Scotland having it constantly blowing across my face quickly becomes an irritation.

When we arrived in Drymen to set off on the Rob Roy Way, the weather was warm but windy and I realised I had forgotten to buy the hairband. Now I was going to have to walk all day and hope that there was a suitable shop in the locality of our overnight accommodation. Much to my surprise, though, I had barely walked 20 metres when I spotted a small purple hairband on the pavement in front of me. It looked pristine. It was the perfect size for my hair. I picked it up and smiled heavenward. My loving father hadn't forgotten what I needed, and he'd placed it there for me – right at the start of the walk. How amazing, and what a fabulous reminder of how he loves us. Not even the smallest of details about our lives escapes his notice.

The secular world constantly focuses on lack, and invites us to partner with a fear that there isn't enough. We live in a society where it is not only acceptable to hoard for the future, it is considered wisdom. As I write this chapter, the news this week has been full of Brexit fears about the danger of Britain not having enough food, medicine and vital supplies in the future. Companies are reportedly stockpiling goods in order to survive this looming disaster.

As administrators we need to balance spirit-led wisdom – think of Joseph preparing for a prophesied famine in Egypt – against an incorrect belief that God is not capable of providing for us, or that, for some mean-spirited reason, he simply won't.

There are many scriptures that speak of God's generosity. It is an inherent part of His character. Here are just a handful:

> If you then, being evil, know how to give good gifts to your children, how much more will your Father who is in heaven give what is good to those who ask Him!
>
> (Matthew 7 verse 11)

> The thief comes only to steal and kill and destroy; I came that they may have life, and have it abundantly.
>
> (John 10 verse 10)

And my God will supply all your needs according to His riches in glory in Christ Jesus.

(Philippians 4 verse 19)

He split the rocks in the wilderness. And gave them abundant drink like the ocean depths.

(Psalm 78 verse 15)

As John 10 verse 10 warns us, the enemy comes to steal, kill and destroy. One of the strategies he will attempt to use is to persuade us to believe the lie that God is not a good and generous father. It is vitally important that we hold fast to the truth because believing the opposite will lead us into self-sabotage.

The volunteer shortage

Let's get practical for a moment and consider an area that many administrators struggle with: recruiting and retaining volunteers. If we truly believe that God will supply all our needs, then that includes the provision of people resources. How often, though, do we approach volunteer recruitment with an expectation of failure? We can all come up with lots of reasons as to why we think people will say no to volunteering as well as having to deal with our own issues about asking people to help.

First, we need to change the way we think and speak. Swapping 'needy' language for a more positive approach where we talk about opportunities is a good starting point. Rather than thinking that the key aim of volunteer recruitment is to get people to work for us (for free!) it is much more positive to consider the key aim as enabling people to have a sense of their God-given purpose. When we talk to people about opportunities to serve we can highlight the joy of living with a purpose and impacting lives for eternity. We need to see that we are giving to people, not taking from them, because the aim is to connect them to their God-given purpose, not simply to connect them to our latest project or slot them into the hole that we need filling.

Bear in mind that this approach is not just a manipulative gimmick. It is alignment with the way Jesus spoke.

> I no longer call you servants, because a servant does not know his master's business. Instead, I have called you friends, for everything that I learned from my Father I have made known to you.
>
> (John 15 verse 15)

These days I nearly always start conversations about serving with questions about what the person concerned enjoys doing, as well as keeping a look out for what I observe them enjoying. For example, I am currently on the lookout for people who can provide an excellent welcome on a Sunday morning. A particular young man had been mentioned to me as a possible leader in this area so I arranged to meet up with him. As we chatted it quickly became apparent that he has a passion for seeing young people growing in their relationship with God. Unsurprisingly he had already started to volunteer with the youth team on a Sunday morning. He had already found his purpose, and I definitely didn't want to encourage him to move from that into the area where I have a number of gaps just to solve my current need. Had I opened the conversation by telling him about the need in the welcome area, it is possible I could have persuaded him to take on the role, but that would not have been ideal for anyone. Instead I will continue to meet up with other people and also keep an eye out on Sundays for those who naturally provide a warm welcome because that is how they are wired.

It is also important to impart vision when recruiting. Consider these two questions:

❏ Would you like to make a real difference on a Sunday morning by encouraging people to build community together?

❏   Would you like to join the refreshment team?

Which question would you say yes to? Or at least be interested in finding out more about what is involved?

On the surface being part of the refreshment team can seem fairly unimportant. Making and serving tea and coffee can appear to be a very mundane task. However, the time that people spend together chatting over a cup of coffee at the end of the service is a key part of community building. That is the moment when friendships begin to form, when people can care for one another, encourage one another, and have those important moments of connection. Our church vision is to be a community that loves God and loves people. Serving on the refreshment team is a key part of enabling that vision to be a reality – it is so much more than simply making tea and coffee.

❏ Are there areas in which you need to change how you think?

Trusting God in all circumstances

Paul, writing to the Philippians, closes his letter with thanks for their provision for him, but goes on to say:

> I have learned to be content whatever the circumstances. I know what it is to be in need, and I know what it is to have plenty. I have learned the secret of being content in any and every situation, whether well fed or hungry, whether living in plenty or in want. I can do all this through him who gives me strength.

> (Philippians 4 verses 11 to 13)

Being able to trust God in every situation is indeed the secret of contentment. One of the areas that I constantly battle with is the middle of the night stress where my mind seems determined to chew on the things that I don't have rather than focusing on the positives. Contentment is notably absent. There is no room for it because all the space is being taken up by worry and anxiety.

There is a declaration that I've found to be extremely valuable at times like this. It is based on Mark 11 verses 22 to 24, where Jesus says:

Have faith in God. Truly I tell you, if anyone says to this mountain, 'Go, throw yourself into the sea,' and does not doubt in their heart but believes that what they say will happen, it will be done for them. Therefore I tell you, whatever you ask for in prayer, believe that you have received it, and it will be yours.

The declaration is this:

I speak to every mountain of discouragement, stress, depression, and lack, and cast it into the sea in Jesus' name.

Try it next time you are feeling discouraged because of a sense of lack. I pray it will bless you as much as it has blessed me.

A land of milk and honey

One of the things I have come to appreciate is the importance of reading Scripture and trying to understand it not only through the lens of modern-day life, but also in the context in which it was written and originally read. I attempt to mentally put myself in their place, both culturally and geographically, and view the words of Scripture through that lens. I recently came across a fascinating discussion of Psalm 23 that highlighted this truth that a Bible passage can look significantly different when viewed from a cultural and geographical perspective than if viewed simply through a contemporary filter.

If you've ever looked at pictures of Israel you may get the impression that its terrain is largely desert-like. Certainly my mental images of Israel tend towards that concept. However, in the Bible Israel is referred to as the land flowing with milk and honey. While this description provides a spiritual picture of a land that flows with God's provision, this phrase is also an illustration of the geography and topography of the land. The land of honey is a reference to the area suitable for farming, of crops and, therefore, bees. This is the area in the west. It runs from the Judean mountains to the foothills and the coastal plain. This is a lush yet relatively small area that is important for providing food for the people of Israel. The land of milk is a reference to the domain of the shepherd. This is the area from the Judean mountains eastward. This is arid wilderness, a land not suitable to grow crops, but sufficient to sustain flocks of sheep and goats. Due to the relatively small amount of farmland, herds would not graze where food for the people was being grown. Thus a land of milk and a land of honey.

The job of the shepherd is to lead his sheep to those areas that can provide the food and water necessary for sustenance. This food is not always easy to find, but a good shepherd knows what to look for. In the cool of the night, when the wind blows from the west off the Mediterranean Sea, moisture condenses against the rocks and provides the water necessary for small tufts of grass to grow. However, by afternoon, the heat of the sun scorches the grass, causing it to wither and die. The shepherd must lead his sheep to these small tufts of grass while they can provide the nourishment the sheep need. These sheep are completely dependent on the shepherd to lead them to this sustenance, each and every day.

It is this skill of the shepherd to provide for the flock that Psalm 23 refers to when it says 'The Lord is my Shepherd. I lack nothing.'

❒ Are you trusting the shepherd to lead you to sustenance? Or are you desperately trying to find resources in the desert in your own strength?

The forbidden phrase

As I mentioned earlier, I have been very challenged by the teaching of Craig Groeschel who leads Life.Church, the largest church in the United States of America. While browsing through his online teaching on YouTube, I came across a video with the intriguing title of *The forbidden phrase*. What phrase could Craig possibly ban his staff, including his many administrators, from saying?

The answer is simple. It is variations on statements that begin with either:

Our people don't ...

or

Our people won't ...

I was immediately convicted on a personal level and also recalled a conversation I'd had with a team leader just a couple of days earlier. Where had I used this phrase? I'd complained that 'people *won't* get up to come to an early morning prayer meeting that starts before 9am'.

When we launched ourselves as a multisite church in September 2017, the site I attended (and now lead) began to meet at 10:00am rather than 10:30am. This meant that the hour-long pre-church prayer meeting moved from 9:00am to 8:30am. Attendance plunged from 20 to 30 people to six or seven on a good morning. Worse still was that of the handful that did come, at least four of them were attending because we require those in key leadership roles on Sundays, such as the meeting host, to be at the prayer meeting.

So I complained that 'people won't attend', and we batted around some ideas and decided to move the prayer meeting back to 9:00am and cut the content down to 30 minutes. On the surface it seems this is working. Attendance has crept back up to

16 to 18 people. (Pockets of prayer also take place around the building as serving teams gather.)

Craig points out that whenever we use the phrase 'people won't ...' or 'people don't ...' we have a choice. We can make an excuse that justifies the statement – in this case that the meeting is too early in the morning – or we can make a difference and admit that the underlying issue is actually that we have not led people into attending the early morning prayer meeting.

He goes on to say that a great leader never places blame on others. Instead a great leader always takes responsibility. As administrators it can be all too tempting to point a finger of blame at others, to whine and complain about 'their' behaviour, and often to throw in the towel because we can't get them to do what we want. Whatever we are complaining about is just the way it is and we have to live with it.

Instead of embracing this defeatist attitude, Craig recommends three practical things that can make a difference.

1. Communicate the why

2. Celebrate the successes

3. Personally set the standard

Communicating the why is vitally important, and also the area that we, as administrators, are most likely to overlook. We tend to be task-focused so we are generally really good at communicating what needs doing and how to do it. If we forget to communicate the why, however, people will feel disengaged and uninspired. No one is going to turn up for a meeting if they don't understand its purpose and have a good reason to attend. Communicating the why connects people to vision and mission. It inspires them to make an effort to attend and be involved. It is also key to understanding what needs doing and how it should be done – without the why it is easy to fall into the trap and put time and effort into the wrong thing.

We also need to be persistent in repeating the why message over and over. Have you ever stopped to think about the number of messages battling for space in your brain on any given day? It must be thousands, and is probably tens of thousands. Take a moment to review a typical day – radio, television, Facebook, Twitter, Whatsapp, advertising hoardings, special offers in the shops, work emails, personal emails, text messages, phone calls, and hopefully plenty of face-to-face conversations with people. We are bombarded with a deluge of information. The only way to keep our message floating on the surface is to constantly dredge it out of the morass and get it back into people's centre of attention.

So for me to communicate the why of our early morning prayer meetings I need to be constantly communicating it to those who attend. If people forget the why and start attending out of habit they will soon become disengaged. I also need to communicate the why on a regular basis to those who don't yet attend. They will never come along if all they know about the prayer meeting is the date, time and venue.

Celebrating success is also another important key to changing a culture of won't to will. We are all wired with a desire to belong, and who doesn't want to be on a winning team? (Or in the case of sports, to be known as an active supporter of the winning team!) So along with communicating the why, it is also really good to communicate success stories.

And finally, we need to personally set the standard. We can't expect other people to do something that we don't. And while it might be tempting to argue that we are 'behind the scenes' people and that a measure of success for administration is that it isn't seen, it remains a fact that how we behave will influence others. Besides, if I'm not at the early morning prayer meeting, how much weight will my exhortation to others to attend carry? Zilch!

Remember too that what we tolerate will dominate. Take for example, tidiness in a general office. If the office manager keeps their own desk spick and span then that models the desired behaviour. He or she is personally setting the standard. However, it needs to go further than that. If the office manager doesn't comment when a volunteer leaves a workspace untidy at the end of a session, guess which desk will start to dominate the environment. By saying nothing the manager has given permission to everyone else to operate at a lower standard. Setting the standard is not just about what we do, but what we require of those in our sphere of influence.

So, when did you last use a phrase that began with 'People won't ...' or 'People don't ...'?

❐ What do you need to communicate to lead people into the desired response?

❐ What are the success stories in this area? (Note: even the smallest of successes is a step in the right direction!)

❐ How can you personally set the standard?

❐ In which areas have you are you tolerating less than the desired standard?

Avoiding the pit of despair

Have you ever had days when it all seems too hard and you just want to throw in the towel and give up? Even the strongest of people can be tempted to wallow in a pit of despair, and particularly so when the demands being placed upon us seem far larger than our mental and physical resources can handle. Take Moses for example. As he leads the Israelites through the wilderness he is constantly having to deal with their complaints.

By Chapter 11 of Numbers it has all become too much for him. The Israelites are tired of eating the manna that God is providing and are whining to Moses that they want meat. Verses 10 to 15 reveal Moses as a man who has, quite simply, had enough.

> Moses heard the people of every family wailing at the entrance to their tents. The LORD became exceedingly angry, and Moses was troubled. He asked the LORD, "Why have you brought this trouble on your servant? What have I done to displease you that you put the burden of all these people on me? Did I conceive all these people? Did I give them birth? Why do you tell me to carry them in my arms, as a nurse carries an infant, to the land you promised on oath to their ancestors? Where can I get meat for all these people? They keep wailing to me, 'Give us meat to eat!' I cannot carry all these people by myself; the burden is too heavy for me. If this is how you are going to treat me, please go ahead and kill me—if I have found favour in your eyes—and do not let me face my own ruin."

What can we learn from this?

First, don't let emotions lead to wrong beliefs. Exhausted and stressed, Moses incorrectly assumes the problems facing him are due to God being displeased with him. To paraphrase his words, he is essentially asking what he has done to deserve the situation. In his mind it is all about himself. What was actually true was that God was angry with the people who were an ungrateful crowd of whinge bags, but there is nothing to suggest that he was displeased with Moses or his leadership.

❒ Are you taking on the blame for something that is not your fault? If so, let it go.

Second, he had taken on more responsibility than God had actually given him. It is true that he had been entrusted to lead a huge crowd of people through very difficult terrain. However, at no point had God asked him to 'carry them … as a nurse carries an infant'. His protest that he cannot carry all the people by himself is based on another false belief that has crept into his mind. He has taken on a huge responsibility and then, in his mind, multiplied it to the point of impossibility.

This is an easy trap to fall into as administrators. We take on a task and before we realise it we have also taken on the belief that we are somehow responsible for the individual happiness of everyone in the church. We are not called to carry people as though they are infants any more than Moses was.

❒ Have you taken on responsibilities that are not yours to bear? If so, hand them back to God.

Third, he was looking to his own resources for the solution rather than God. As he demands to know where he is going to get meat for all these people, he is not asking in an expectation that God will provide, but rather as a complaint at his own lack of resource. Despite all he had seen God do in the past, and despite the promises God had made to him, all he can see in his future is failure, and he informs God that he would rather die than face that. He had come to the end of himself and wanted out. Even when God says he will provide meat, not just for one day but for an entire month, Moses is not placated. He throws a bad-tempered response back. Where is this meat going to come from? How can there possibly be meat for all these people.

It is then that God reminds Moses about who he is addressing. 'Is the Lord's arm too short?' God says. The question is a reminder to Moses of God's strength and of all he has already done. It refocuses Moses attention from his own frailty and lack to the power and faithfulness of God. With God there is always enough. In this case, it was the provision of quail meat.

When we find ourselves overwhelmed, exhausted and stressed it is good to turn to Psalm 121 which contains a useful reminder to keep our focus on God in its eight verses.

I lift up my eyes to the mountains -
where does my help come from?
My help comes from the LORD,
the Maker of heaven and earth.

He will not let your foot slip—
he who watches over you will not slumber;
indeed, he who watches over Israel
will neither slumber nor sleep.

The LORD watches over you—
the LORD is your shade at your right hand;
the sun will not harm you by day,
nor the moon by night.

The LORD will keep you from all harm—
he will watch over your life;
the LORD will watch over your coming and going
both now and forevermore.

❏ Are you facing a situation in which you feel inadequate with nothing but potential failure ahead? Lift your eyes to the Lord. His arm is not too short.

Grapes or giants?

There is one more lesson to draw on from Moses' experience in the wilderness. In Numbers 13 the Israelites are drawing close to Canaan, the land God has promised to give to them. Moses is instructed to send 12 men to spy out the land and report back. They are told where to go and what to do.

When Moses sent them to explore Canaan, he said, "Go up through the Negev and on into the hill country. See what the land is like and whether the people who live there are strong or weak, few or many. What kind of land do they live in? Is it good or bad? What kind of towns do they live in? Are they unwalled or fortified? How is the soil? Is it fertile or poor? Are there trees in it or not? Do your best to bring back some of the fruit of the land. (It was the season for the first ripe grapes.)

(Numbers 13 verses 17 to 20)

Forty days later the men return. Two of them return with a cluster of grapes as well as pomegranates and figs. They report both good news and bad. The good is that the land was indeed flowing with milk and honey. The bad is that 'the people who live there are powerful and the cities are fortified and very large'. However, focusing on the promise of God to give them the land they urge the people to take the land, stating that 'we can do it'.

Unfortunately not all the spies had focused on grapes. The others magnified the problems, focusing on the fact that there were giants in the land. We can't take this land, they protested 'we seemed like grasshoppers in our own eyes, and we looked the same to them'. If only they had held onto the truth that 'God can do all things'.

❏ Are you focusing on grapes or giants?

Here is a declaration that draws on the truth in Ephesians 3 verse 20. It is one that I've found helpful when tempted to look at the giants rather than celebrate the presence of grapes.

> I speak to this day, and I call you blessed. I declare I serve a mighty God who today will do exceedingly and abundantly beyond all that I can ask or think. I say You are a good God and I eagerly anticipate Your goodness today.

I encourage you to write it somewhere that is visible in your workplace. Then the next time the giants seem to be looming over everything use it to put them in their place. Our Father is much bigger, and he is also generous and loving, and willing to provide all our needs.

Stewarding well in abundance

Having focused on the various challenges of a lack of resources – whether real or anticipated – let's briefly look at the other side of the coin. How do we steward well in abundance?

A grateful heart

A pastor from an African nation recently told the story of a woman in his church who came to him in a state of anxiety. Her husband had built a new house for her. It was everything she had longed for in terms of size and location. There was, however, a major problem with it. Every time she stayed in the house she fell ill. When she left the house she would recover her health. Clearly the house was cursed. She begged the pastor to come to the house and pray over it.

The pastor agreed he would pray into the problem. However, when he did God revealed the true source of the problem. And so he arranged to meet with the woman again.

'I have good news for you,' he told her. 'God has shown me the reason for your ill health.'

'Praise the Lord,' the woman responded. 'Tell me what you will do to break the curse.'

The pastor shook his head. 'There is nothing I can do. The Lord revealed to me that the reason for your ill health whenever you stay in the house comes from your lack of gratitude. He told me you have never thanked him for his provision of the house. In fact, you secretly wish that it was a bit bigger and set in a larger piece of land.'

The woman turned pale, and then confessed. 'What you say is true. I was not completely satisfied with the house. I did secretly want more.' Her eyes filled with tears. 'I have brought this on myself, haven't I?'

The pastor nodded and invited her to repent of her lack of gratitude. She then returned to the house and lived in it without further ill health.

This story illustrates one of the pitfalls awaiting us in times of abundance – a lack of gratitude for what God has given us. And while it was told by a pastor from Africa, we all need to be on guard, particularly in the Western world because the culture leans heavily towards one of entitlement. Just think of the strapline of a premium brand of shampoo that reinforces this every time it tells potential customers to buy their product because 'you're worth it'.

1 Thessalonians 5 verse 18 reminds us to give thanks in all circumstances. Let's remember to do that in times of abundance. When we remind ourselves that what we have comes from God, it draws our minds back to the truth that what we are doing is for his glory. Our role as administrators is not primarily about big buildings or big gatherings of people. It is about bringing glory to the King of Kings.

❏ Are there things in your life that you have taken for granted? Take some time now to thank Father God for his blessing and favour.

Too much choice

Have you ever walked down the aisle of a supermarket in search of a particular product and been so overwhelmed by the range on offer you've felt paralysed as to which item to buy? Sometimes having lots of options to choose from can bring anxiety rather than freedom, and we just want someone to rescue us from indecision and to tell us what to do.

Too much choice can also lead us into fearing that we will miss out if we make the wrong decision – that we might choose something that is second-best. Perhaps this is why there is a growing trend for people to not reply to invitations to events until the last minute. Something better might come along and if they have already accepted an invitation then they will either miss out or have that awkward situation of wanting to now decline the earlier invitation without offending the host.

As I mentioned earlier, sometimes the outpouring of God's favour on us manifests itself in an abundance of opportunities. It is a recognition that we are his friends, not slaves, and so he trusts us to make choices. He delights in treating us as adults, not as children who must be directed step by step through every minute of the day.

So how do we avoid being paralysed by too much choice?

In the 2004 book *The Paradox of Choice: Why More is Less*, the American psychologist Barry Schwartz suggests there are five steps to follow for good decision-making:

1. **Figure out your goal or goals** – or in other words, what do you want? If you are choosing a movie, for example, it might be that you want to have a laugh or you might be looking for a movie that challenges you intellectually. Or perhaps you are in the thrill-seeking mood and want a story that will give you an adrenaline rush.
2. **Evaluate the importance of each goal.** If you are choosing a movie you may be happy to base your choice on the recommendation of a friend. If you are buying a car you may seek advice from a friend, but you are also most likely to do further in-depth research before parting with your cash.
3. **Assemble the options.** If you want to spend an evening at the cinema with friends you may have a range of movies that would adequately serve your goal. If you specifically want to see a thriller, your options will likely be more limited.
4. **Evaluate the options.** If one of your friend hates costume dramas a movie set in Victorian times is unlikely to be a good choice for a harmonious evening at the cinema.

5. Pick the option that has the best fit with your goal.

These five steps use everyday decisions as examples, but they also apply to the more important decisions in life. I know of a young couple who are getting married very soon. They were not living in the same town when they met so their first decision was regarding location. Having made that choice, they are now trying to decide which of the two sites of New Life Church to attend as a newly married couple. Both sites are good options, and there really isn't a right or wrong choice. God is blessing them with options, and I am confident he will bless them wherever they go.

It is also important to keep remembering verse 11 from Jeremiah 29:

> For I know the plans I have for you," declares the LORD, "plans to prosper you and not to harm you, plans to give you hope and a future.

I remember when my husband and I moved to Milton Keynes and we began to visit churches there were a number of really good options. We ended up at New Life Church not because we felt God strongly directed us there but rather because I walked in the door and felt at home. I was expecting my second child and a number of women in the congregation were also expecting babies. My husband also felt a sense of peace that this was the right place for us, even though he had a friend in a church much closer to our home. We can honestly say that God has prospered us through the church. There have been good times and difficult times in our lives, but throughout it all, the family of New Life has been a great blessing to us.

So, when choices arise in life let's not be paralysed by the fear that we might make the wrong decision. Rather we should thank God for his abundant blessing, consider the desires that he has put in our heart, seek wise counsel if we feel we need it, and then step into the future knowing he will prosper us.

A prayer for decision making

Father God

I thank you that you that you have plans for me and that you go before me so that I may have hope and a future.

I thank you that you are not a dictatorial father, but rather you lead me gently and sometimes lay before me a feast of choices.

I declare that I will not be paralysed by the analysis of the choices before me, nor will I fear missing out on other options. I thank you for the skills and gifts you have given me, and for the desires and dreams that you have placed within me.

May I partner with you in all that I do, to bring glory to your name.

Amen

References

Schwartz, B. (2004) *The Paradox of Choice: Why More is Less*, Harper Collins, New York.

Chapter 5 God loves systems

To understand God's thoughts we must study statistics, for these are the measure of his purpose.

(attributed to Florence Nightingale[1])

Uncovering his hidden systems

Did you know that God loves systems? Yes, really! He absolutely loves them. How can we know this? Take a look at his creation. The universe is a set of systems. Matter is spreading outwards. It is coalescing into planets. It is imploding as solar systems die. Not only that, but our universe is a highly tuned system. There are a number of constants in physics that have to be finely tuned to an extreme level for the universe to be suitable for life to exist. Stephen Hawking comments on this in his book *A Brief of History of Time* (Hawking, 1988, p. 7) saying: 'The remarkable fact is that the values of these numbers seem to have been very finely adjusted to make possible the development of life.'

---

[1] There is some debate as to whether these words were Florence Nightingale's own or attributed to her. There is, however, no question regarding her championing statistics and their use. In 1858, she was the first woman to be elected as a Fellow of the Statistical Society of London, and was also elected to the Statistical Congress. In 1874 she was made an honorary foreign member of the American Statistical Association (Magnello, E., 2010).

One of these values is the ratio of electrons to protons. The number of electrons has to be equivalent to the number of protons with an accuracy of $1:10^{37}$ to prevent electromagnetic forces in the universe overcoming gravitational forces. Without this finely tuned balance the galaxies, stars, and planets never would have formed. It is hard to visualise what that means but Dr. Hugh Ross gives it a go in his book, *The Creator and the Cosmos*:

> Cover the entire North American continent in dimes all the way up to the moon, a height of about 239,000 miles. (In comparison, the money to pay for the U.S. federal government debt would cover one square mile less than two feet deep with dimes.) Next, pile dimes from here to the moon on a billion other continents the same size as North America. Paint one dime red and mix it into the billions of piles of dimes. Blindfold a friend and ask him to pick out one dime. The odds that he will pick the red dime are one in 10^{37}.

(Ross, 2001, p. 115)

Then there are human beings – you and me. We are a set of systems – respiratory, circulatory, nervous, reproductive, and so on. We also know that we are made in the image of God so we can reasonably conclude that God is a set of systems as well. That's a bit mind-blowing isn't it?

There are many other systems in the natural world. It is also worth noting that whenever we read of the kingdom of God moving forward in the Bible there's a significant systematic organisational element. In the Book of Numbers Moses organised his leaders to oversee 1000s and 100s, and there are divisions into families, clans and tribes. In Acts 6 we read about deacons serving in the church to free up the apostles – they were the system people who ensured the widows and orphans were taken care of.

As administrators we are wired to understand and think systems, and so it is really good news that God loves them. If you are ever tempted to think that no one else understands what you are doing or that no one has an appreciation of the carefully crafted system you've introduced to make things run smoothly, you can remind yourself that God appreciates you and what you are doing because he is really into systems!

It is also good to remember that, just as God knows how many hairs each of us have on our heads, he also knows all the details of even the most complicated systems, including the trillions of computer programs that make our modern world function.

Helen was a computer programmer who worked for a well-known retail chain before her retirement in 2019. One day she and her team were faced with a program that wasn't working correctly. Somewhere in the thousands of lines of code there was an error that was defying the usual debugging routines. The only way to track it down was by manually checking each line of code. The task was enormous, and incredibly tedious. Helen, however, had a light bulb moment. God knew the content of the entire program and he knew exactly where the error was hiding. So rather than join in the manual search she prayed for revelation. God directed her to a specific piece of the code, and sure enough there was the error. Her work colleagues were amazed that she had found it so quickly – and more than a bit bemused when she explained how.

In all things related to administration, let's always remember that God is omnipotent. He knows everything, and he is ready and willing to help us if we ask.

Nehemiah and a systems thinking approach

Systems are often highly complex, and if you change one element of a system it can have a massive impact somewhere else in the system. Think again about the ratio of electrons to protons – an infinitesimally minute change to the ratio could end life as we know it. Peter Senge, who popularised the concept of systems thinking likens systems to families:

Whenever I'm trying to help people understand what this word 'system' means, I usually start by asking: 'Are you a part of a family?' Everybody is a part of a family. 'Have you ever seen in a family, people producing consequences in the family, how people act, how people feel, that aren't what anybody intends?' Yes. 'How does that happen?' Well... then people tell their stories and think about it. But that then grounds people in not the jargon of 'system' or 'systems thinking' but the reality – that we live in webs of interdependence.

(Senge, 2014, YouTube)

The essence of systems thinking and practice is in 'seeing' the world in a particular way, because how you 'see' things affects the way you approach situations or undertake specific tasks. Peter Senge wrote in his book *The Fifth Discipline*: 'Systems thinking is a discipline for seeing wholes. It is a framework for seeing interrelationships rather than things, for seeing patterns of change rather than static "snapshots"' (Senge, 1990, p. 68)

For a Biblical example of how this can work let's look again at the story of Nehemiah. He demonstrated the ability to solve a complex problem – rebuilding the walls of Jerusalem. Two elements of systems thinking that Senge refers to as The Fifth Discipline made a difference for Nehemiah: 'the subtle interconnectedness that gives living systems their unique character' and the '"structures" that underlie complex situations' (p. 69). Also Nehemiah asked God to help him in the task.

In Nehemiah 2 verses 1 to 9 nothing overtly miraculous occurs. There is no turning of water into wine or lost axe heads floating on the water. Instead these verses outline a logical approach to a problem and the steps Nehemiah took to get things under way. First of all he understood where the power lay – with the king – but he also knew that a direct approach was not the way to go, rather he needed the king to initiate a conversation with him. This he achieved through his demeanour.

In the month of Nisan...the king asked me, "Why does your face look so sad when you are not ill? This can be nothing but sadness of heart."

I was very much afraid, but I said to the king, "May the king live forever! Why should my face not look sad when the city where my fathers are buried lies in ruins, and its gates have been destroyed by fire?"

The king said to me, "What is it you want?"

Having achieved the first step of having an opportunity to ask for what he wanted, he then asks for God's favour and makes his request. Note, also, he was prepared for the next step – setting a timescale for his project.

Then I prayed to the God of heaven, and I answered the king, "If it pleases the king and if your servant has found favour in his sight, let him send me to the city of Judah where my fathers are buried so that I can rebuild it...."

It pleased the king to send me; so I set a time.

Next we see just how well Nehemiah has thought things through. He requests letters from various key players without whom he cannot achieve his goal. Everything he asked for he received, and because he had also sought God's favour on his plans he got more than he asked for. The king threw in a bunch of army officers and cavalry as well.

I also said to him, "If it pleases the king, may I have letters to the governors of Trans-Euphrates, so that they will provide me safe-conduct until I arrive in Judah? And may I have a letter to Asaph, keeper of the king's forest, so he will give me timber to make beams for the gates of the citadel by the temple and for the city wall and for the residence I will occupy?" And because the gracious hand of my God was upon me, the king granted my requests. So I went to the governors of Trans-Euphrates and gave them the king's letters. The king had also sent army officers and cavalry with me.

Nehemiah was so successful in thinking through the way the system worked and the processes he needed to get into place that, when people saw it, "they realized that this work had been done with the help of [their] God" (Nehemiah 6 verse 16). Nehemiah's ability to solve complex problems grew out of his manner of seeing the problems from the perspective of a systems thinker. And what we see in this story is hard work, good leadership and the hand of God.

From systems to processes

If you can't describe what you are doing as a process, then you don't know what you are doing.

(Professor W. Edwards Deming)

Every system is made up of processes, the related activities that work together to make the system function. I recently attended a two-day training event on church growth that was an absolute delight in terms of emphasising the importance of the gift of administration. The leaders of two large churches shared their stories and passed on invaluable insights into the lessons they had learnt and how things operated behind the scenes. It quickly became apparent that these leaders have a process for everything. Without processes, church life – which is a large-scale system - quickly becomes inefficient and chaotic.

Actually there is a process behind everything we do. Take a moment to consider how you make a cup of instant coffee.

- Put water in a kettle and bring to the boil.

- Fetch the following items from their storage places: cup/mug, teaspoon, jar of coffee and, if required, milk, sugar.

- Place appropriate amounts of coffee, sugar and milk in the cup/mug.

- Add boiling water, stir and drink.

You may already be thinking that the process outlined above is wrong or incomplete. Some people put milk in the mug before the water, some add it after. Some people would argue that the water should be hot but not boiling. If you want to improve the efficiency of the process you might have realised that – as in my kitchen – having mugs in a cupboard at the opposite end of the kitchen to everything else is not the optimum storage location. The process of making something as simple as a cup of instant coffee is actually quite complex when you break it down into its component steps.

This example also demonstrates that every task has an underlining process, even if we are not consciously aware of it. Recognising that fact is often a vital first step. It is also key for countering protests that a task doesn't require a process.

Now, most of us probably aren't too concerned about the efficiency of making coffee in our own homes. However, most churches provide tea and coffee for their congregations on a Sunday morning. Efficiency becomes much more important when tens or hundreds of cups of coffee need to be prepared and ready for consumption at a given time. A good process is not only vital, it is also important to review it regularly.

So if processes are important how do we go about ensuring we have good processes in place? The answer is to conduct a process audit. Many of us will groan inwardly at the idea of doing this. Isn't it just one more time-consuming thing to add to the to-do list? It is true, it will need time, but the benefits are likely to far outweigh the alternative, which is to muddle along with undefined and possibly inefficient processes.

Seeking the Goldilocks zone

Before we get into the how, let's focus a little longer on the why? What do we want to achieve through the audit process.

Are you familiar with the story of Goldilocks and the three bears? At each stage in the story – let's gloss over her anti-social behaviour – she tried out various things in the house and for each element, e.g. the bowls of porridge, she rejected two and declared one to be 'just right'. The aim of a process audit is identify processes that need to be fine-tuned to make them 'just right'.

Processes should help the teams who are using them. They need to be the right size – not too big, not too small. They need to allow for flexibility – if a process is too rigid it may stifle creativity. They need to be open to challenge because you may be surprised who on the team has spotted something that can bring about improvement. And, of course, sometimes it can be someone looking in from the outside who spots a way to tighten up efficiency or take a completely different approach to how something is being done.

A young man recently moved to Milton Keynes and started attending the Sunday services at the site I lead. As I knew him to be someone with a good strategic mind and experience of a church similar to New Life I waited for six weeks and then asked him to tell me what he thought we were doing well and anything he had observed where he thought we could bring about improvement. He was complimentary about most of what we do, but he had one particularly helpful comment about the way we explain the use of prophetic contributions. I was delighted to take his feedback on board and change our process. A fresh pair of eyes can be highly valuable.

Planning a process audit

Not surprisingly, the first stage of a process audit is planning. Make a list of all the areas that you want to examine. This will reflect the areas that you are responsible for, which vary considerably from one administrator to another. For example, in my current role I am responsible for human resources, church-wide communication, and the efficient running and spiritual growth of one of our two sites. The area that I currently feel is in need of a process audit is the efficient running of the Sunday morning service at the site I lead. You may want to focus on a different area, perhaps the office processes. Often processes that need auditing are the ones that are causing frustration. Keep your ear to the ground and find out what people are grumbling about.

A couple of years ago the refreshment team was losing volunteers at an unsustainable rate. At that time we served people with tea and coffee from a single servicing point. This had been a perfectly good process when we were a church of around 150, but we were now a church of 300 plus. Serving that many people in a short space of time had become hugely stressful. There was a great deal of grumbling. When we recognised this and gave it some attention we realised the answer was to completely change the process so that we had six self-serve stations around the auditorium. The role of the refreshment team changed to ensuring the stations were set up in a timely manner, kept supplied with milk and coffee after the service, and then cleared away as people departed. I'm pleased to say that the grumbling ceased – at least in that area.

Having identified an area, the next stage is to break it down into manageable chunks. For example, I'm keen to look at the processes involved in welcoming people to our service, so that will be on my list.

As with any task there needs to be a schedule – start date and end dates. In addition, there is a need for the sub-tasks to be identified and scheduled in for auditing too.

Create an audit document

A process audit is essentially a data gathering exercise, but how can you figure out what data to gather and who to gather it from? Businesses often use turtle diagrams (Google this if you are interested). A simple mind map is just as effective. This is a visualisation of the processes that covers all the different things that are involved in them: equipment, supplies, people, etc.

The starting point for an audit document will depend on what is already in place. If you already have a detailed written process for a task then you will probably want to ask the following questions:

- Why are we performing this task? – This is the opportunity to check that a given task still has a valid purpose and isn't simply being done because 'we always do that'.

- Is it being done according to the agreed process? It is surprising how quickly an agreed process is forgotten and people start to make things up as they go along.

- Can it be fine-tuned to make it more effective?

If there isn't an agreed process then two key questions will be:

- What is being done?

- Who is doing it?

The document should include who to talk to – both those who are involved in delivering the process and those who are on the receiving end of it.

Creating an action plan

At the end of the audit process you will be faced with one of two scenarios.

The first is that the process is working pretty well, but you've identified one or two small improvements to make. The next step, therefore, is to create and implement an action plan that will fine-tune the process. You can then sit back and congratulate yourself and your team on a job well done.

The second scenario is more of a challenge. In this case the audit has revealed that the process is in dire need of an overhaul. Nothing is really working the way it was intended. As with our need to completely replace how we delivered refreshments on a

Sunday morning, there is a need to go back to the drawing board and start afresh.

One of the most valuable things we've learnt to do is to be constantly on the lookout for processes that other people are using, and ideally to have ideas waiting in the wings for implementation. In particular we try to look at the processes of other churches that are at least one or two stages ahead of where we are now. We have no desire to 'reinvent the wheel' for ourselves. The great thing about the church community is that we are not alone. With the exception of, perhaps, the really large megachurches of thousands that exist, most of us are following in the footsteps left by another church that is a little bit further down the road. And generally, church communities are very happy to share their experiences with others – both the things that worked and the things that didn't.

This approach proved particularly valuable for us when we felt God was calling us to become a multisite church. We were starting with a blank page – well, blank other than the prophetic calling we had from God – and so we set about researching what others had done before us. We read every book and article we could find on the subject. We attended training events. One run by a large church in Catford proved particularly valuable because their leaders were incredibly open and honest about the pitfalls they had both avoided and fallen into, enabling us to tread a more secure path towards multisite. Little by little we built up a plan and a number of brand new processes that were fine-tuned to our particular circumstances. Throughout the process we remained incredibly grateful to all those who gave us input, advice and wisdom. Not everything translated to our situation, but a vast amount did. As a result, when we relaunched ourselves as a multisite church we encountered few teething problems.

Obviously this research and planning took up a considerable amount of time and effort, but how much more effort might have been used had we tried to fill the blank sheet of paper purely on our own?

❒ Do you have relationship with others who are further down the road than you? If yes, what can you learn from them? If no, how can you develop such relationships?

In some areas, we have also realised there is enormous value in paying for outside expertise. For example, we do not have anyone on staff with human resource expertise, plus this is an area of the law that is constantly changing. As our staff team rapidly expanded we soon became aware that we needed to have strong, robust and legally compliant processes in place. We therefore decided to enter into a contract with a professional HR company that would not only provide good processes for us to follow, they would also do all the hard work of keeping up to date with employment law and provide us with advice on issues as and when we needed it. There is a financial cost to this, but it is far less than having an HR expert on staff. Plus instead of one expert, we have access to a large team of experts who offer 24/7 support.

Gathering the numbers

Benjamin Disraeli, who twice served as the British Prime Minister in the 1800s, famously said there are three kinds of lies – lies, damn lies and statistics. Clearly he was not a fan of the process of collecting data to create statistics.

On the other hand, Florence Nightingale believed that a statistics department was absolutely essential in what she was trying to achieve. During the Crimean War of 1854-6, Florence worked in the Scutari Hospital in Constantinople (now Istanbul). The hospital was in a terrible state when Florence arrived with dirty beds, clogged latrines and bad food. To tackle the situation, she wrote a detailed statistical report that presented five reasons for the high mortality rates in the hospital: overcrowding, lack of ventilation, poor drainage, poor standards of cleanliness and a lack of hospital comforts such as knives and forks for meal times

(Neuhauser, 2003). She quantified and measured each of the problems and her proposed solutions.

When she encountered resistance to change she threatened to publish the report unless the British government created a Royal Commission with the powers to make improvements. She got her own way and the Commission was duly created. A large part of her statistical report can now be read in the 1999 publication *Florence Nightingale: Measuring Hospital Care Outcomes* (JCAHO, 1999). You can also read more about Florence Nightingale's excellent use of statistics in Eileen Magnello's easy-to-read article, *Florence Nightingale: The compassionate statistician*, which is freely available online – see References for details.

Having extolled the mathematical skills of Florence Nightingale I have to confess that I am not a huge fan of the process of data collecting. It fits right down in the dull and tedious end of the spectrum of administrative tasks in my opinion. However, over the years I have come to appreciate the enormous value of statistics for forward planning. As Richard Wightman is fond of saying 'How can you plan anything without knowing the numbers?'

Data collection is not one of the topics that instantly springs to mind when reading the Bible, but the notion that you can't plan anything without knowing the numbers can be drawn from scripture. The Book of Numbers takes its name from the fact that God told Moses to count the people at the start of Israel's forty year journey through the wilderness:

> The LORD spoke to Moses in the tent of meeting in the Desert of Sinai on the first day of the second month of the second year after the Israelites came out of Egypt. He said: "Take a census of the whole Israelite community by their clans and families, listing every man by name, one by one. You and Aaron are to count according to their divisions all the men in Israel who are twenty years old or more and able to serve in the army. One man from each tribe, each of them the head of his family, is to help you.

After the count the Israelites then travelled in well-ordered divisions. Numbers 2 starts by saying:

> The LORD said to Moses and Aaron: "The Israelites are to camp around the tent of meeting some distance from it, each of them under their standard and holding the banners of their family."

It then lists each of the families, names the family leader and gives the number of people in that family. Finally it states in Numbers 2 verse 34

> So the Israelites did everything the LORD commanded Moses; that is the way they encamped under their standards, and that is the way they set out, each of them with their clan and family.

Numbers 3 and 4 also provide an interesting insight into the use of data collection for administrative purposes. If, like many of us, it is a book you generally skip over, take a few moments to read these early chapters and gain a fresh appreciation of the fact that God is the greatest administrator of us all.

So, back in the present, over the years the staff team at New Life Church has underpinned a lot of what we do with data collection, and we have gradually increased our data collection processes. Let's take a quick look at a key set of data: Sunday morning headcount.

Each Sunday morning, about 40 minutes into the service, our stewards make a note of how many adults, youth and children are in the auditorium. On Monday our children and youth leaders provide numbers for those present in their groups around the building. The totals for each of the three age brackets are then recorded in a spreadsheet along with a ten-week rolling average attendance that Excel automatically calculates.

From this simple data collection each week we have been able to track our growth over the past ten years, identify annual and seasonal trends, and most importantly predict future growth. Having the ability to use reliable data to predict the future has been invaluable to us. For example, we could estimate that the pressure on space in our building, before we went multisite, would be on the children's groups meeting in smaller rooms and halls, rather than on adults in the auditorium. We could also estimate that we would run out of space within a year to eighteen months, therefore, that was the time span we had to come up with a solution. The process of finding that solution involved a mix of prayer, strategic thinking, prophecy – God very clearly told us not to go to multiple services – and hard work in turning an idea – a second site located elsewhere in the city – into a reality.

After a year of operating as a multisite church we are watching the statistics carefully and estimating that we are again about two years away from needing to find another space solution. Prayer and strategy is kicking in. We await the prophetic guidance.

❑ What data do you collect on a regular basis and how do you use it to inform decisions?

Data collection and statistics really do form the background for decision making, from minor to major. Here's another example. We have been reviewing our welcome processes and will launch a new first time visitor gift bag in September. We are really excited about this as we have sourced a quality bag printed with our logo and website that we will fill with small gifts and information to make people feel value and loved, and also to provide them with visible reminders of New Life Church. Having done all the research, the key question was how many of each item to order. The answer was simple. We know how many first time visitor packs we have given out over the past year because we've recorded the data. Ordering a year's worth of stock, rather than say six months' worth, was good value for money. In this case our data collection enabled us to make a cost-effective decision.

This year our planning process, which starts in May for a September implementation, included asking all our department leaders to give serious thought to the data that they should collect over the comings months. I confess I expected a bit of groaning and complaint, but very little of that happened because we have all learnt the value of data collection and statistics.

If you are new to data collection do ask other churches what information they collect and how they use it. There are also some excellent resources on the internet.

References

Hawking, S. (1988) *A Brief of History of Time,* Bantam, p. 7.

JCAHO (1999) FLORENCE NIGHTINGALE: MEASURING HOSPITAL CARE OUTCOMES, Joint Commission on Accreditation of Healthcare Organizations, Oakbrook Terrace, Illinois.

Magnello, E. (2010) 'Florence Nightingale: The compassionate statistician', Plus Magazine. Available online at: https://plus.maths.org/content/florence-nightingale-compassionate-statistician Accessed 5 June 2019.

Neuhauser, D. (2003) Florence Nightingale gets no respect: as a statistician that is. Available online at: https://qualitysafety.bmj.com/content/12/4/317. Accessed 25 July 2019.

Ross, H. (2001) *The Creator and the Cosmos*, Colorado Springs, Colorado: Navpress

Senge, P. (1990) The Fifth Discipline, The Art and Practice of the Learning Organisation, Cornerstone.

Senge, p. (2014) Introduction to Systems Thinking, YouTube video. Available online at: https://www.youtube.com/watch?v=eXdzKBWDraM Accessed 5 June 2019.

Chapter 6 When strength becomes weakness

In most cases strengths and weaknesses are two sides of the same coin.
(Steve Jobs)

Ever had a knee-jerk reaction?

It was Easter Sunday morning. Everything was going wonderfully well. The auditorium was packed to the seams. The worship team was in full flow, and people were engaged, singing praises to the risen king. Elsewhere in the building children were celebrating in their various age groups. Upstairs the youth group were worshiping for all they were worth.

And then the fire alarm went off!

It was pretty obvious from where I was standing (on stage hosting the meeting), that there wasn't a fire. And given the fact that our fire sensors are notoriously sensitive to cigarette smoke wafting through the open doors into the reception area, I suspected it was a false alarm. As the stewarding team leapt into action, doing a fast sweep of the building to check if we were indeed safe, I made the judgement to continue with worship. I informed the congregation that we suspected it was a false alarm, and that we were checking this was indeed the case, and if, in a couple of minutes we discovered otherwise we would evacuate the building. Given the number of fire doors in the auditorium we can evacuate a large number of people extremely quickly so I was confident this was a safe, if rather impromptu, risk assessment decision and in line with our fire safety policies.

Sure enough the stewards returned within a couple of minutes and reported all was well in the building. One of the children's groups was celebrating with toasted hot cross buns. The team leader had taken a toaster from the kitchen to the meeting room, filled it with buns and then turned their attention onto something else. As we have probably all experienced, a slice of bun didn't pop up when done, jamming the toaster in the on position, and had started to burn. The resulting smoke set off the alarm.

Easter Sunday continued on, and everyone had a good time. Everyone except for me who informed our senior leader at the end of the meeting that I was banning toasters from the building. This wasn't the first time a toaster had been the cause of setting off the alarm. Just a few days earlier we'd had problems when someone introduced one to the small kitchen area in the general office that staff and volunteers use to make tea and coffee. I was done with toasters. And as the operations manager I had the authority to ban them.

Why am I telling this story? Because it was a moment in which I realised I was in danger of abusing the power I held, and of losing sight of the fact that church is about people, not tasks. One of my strengths as an operations manager is to create processes that enable things to run well and safely. When necessary I also have authority to enforce necessary processes, and indeed for some aspects I am legally required to do so. But that strength becomes a weakness if used to enforce a process that is heavy-handed and detrimental to the operation of the church. Providing toasted treats for our children and young people is part of what we do; it helps to model family and it demonstrates generosity. My desire to ban toasters was a knee-jerk reaction to an unfortunate incident that certainly needed addressing but not that heavily.

A couple of days later, when I'd had time to mentally process things, I sent an email out to all our staff and volunteers asking them to provide continuous monitoring of toasters when using them. I adopted a light-hearted tone that used a reference from the Doctor Who episode featuring weeping angels that caused trouble if people weren't looking at them. A phrase from the show had become popular at the time: Don't blink! The email read something like this:

Dear all. As you may be aware we occasionally have troublesome toasters in operation. These toasters are determined to burn anything you put into them in order to set off the fire alarms. To foil this dastardly plot you are kindly asked to do the following:

- Do not enable the toaster in its determination to burn items by using it on too high a setting. (Remember sugary items burn quickly – use a low setting.)

- Do not leave toasters unattended. Do not walk away. Do not turn your back to them.

- Do not blink!

It was one of the most well-received emails I've ever sent. It made people laugh, but it also made the point. The person responsible for burning hot cross buns on Easter Sunday apologised profusely. And, most important of all, I don't recall us having any further issues with toasters!

Two sides of the same coin

Often our biggest strength is also our biggest weakness. I have become more and more aware of the truth of this statement as I've moved into managing people. You may also be aware of it in the people you interact with, not only at work but in life in general.

A couple of weeks ago I had a routine dental appointment. As I sat in the waiting room and watched the hands on the clock crawl past my appointment time, I began to think less than kindly about my dentist. This wasn't the first time I had been left sitting on a hard chair with nothing to do but browse an old copy of the Reader's Digest for fifteen minutes or more. And besides my appointment was for 9:30am and the surgery started at 9:00am. How could she be running so late so soon? From the arrival and departure of other patients for other dentists, punctuality clearly wasn't a problem for others.

Finally I got called in to see her. She apologised for her tardiness and set about the routine check I had booked. I mentioned the filling that had fallen out of a back tooth since I last saw her, fully expecting to be told to make another appointment for treatment. But no. She didn't want me to put up with the problem longer than necessary and said she could fix it right now if I was willing to let her do so. Instantly my opinion of her changed. I was delighted to walk out of the surgery with a repaired tooth. Of course, making the repair took a little longer than the fifteen minutes allocated to a routine check-up. The patient after me was no doubt sitting in the waiting room glowering at the clock just as I had been earlier.

My dentist has a number of strengths including compassion for her patients. But that strength is also a weakness because it causes her to focus on the needs of the patient in the chair at the expense of those waiting to be seen.

As administrators we need to be on the lookout for our strengths also being our weaknesses.

❒ What are your strengths?

❒ How can your strengths morph into weaknesses?

Let's explore some of the ways we can get tripped up in this area. You may recognise yourself in these scenarios. If so, don't feel condemned and beat yourself up. Rather put your wonderful administrative skills to work in coming up with a plan to avoid getting tripped up in the future. If you don't recognise yourself then well done. Do, however, remain on guard. These things can sneak up on us when we least expect it. I keep thinking that I have my identity in Christ firmly sorted, but this week, once again, I found the orphan-hearted version of me is still alive and kicking.

Let's look at the story of Martha (Luke 10 verses 38 to 42). I rather like Martha because for years I managed to use activity to mask shyness around people, particularly in large groups. I would much rather be chopping vegetables in the kitchen than attempting to make conversation with people at a party.

Luke tells us that when Jesus visited Martha's home in Bethany she was engaged in a whirlwind of domestic activity while her sister Mary simply sat and listened to Jesus talk.

You can probably imagine the amount of work that was needed to welcome Jesus and his disciples. The house would need a clean and there would be some work involved in making a small abode comfortable and welcoming for a large group. Martha may have run around her neighbours borrowing what she needed: extra platters, more drinking vessels, perhaps some additional cushions and rugs. Her visitors would also need water to wash their feet after their journey – as custom demanded - and she would need plenty more water for cooking. This would require at least one visit to the local well, and perhaps several depending on the size and shape of the water jars Martha owned or had borrowed. Food would need to be purchased, then prepared, cooked and served. This was no small snack for a passing visitor, and she couldn't nip to the local shop for ready-prepared meals or order in a pile of pizzas. Everything had to be made from scratch, including the bread – a staple part of most meals. Martha had at least 13 extra people coming for dinner. Most of them were ordinary men, but they had been out all day and so would almost certainly be very hungry. This meant she needed to cook generous amounts. And then there was Jesus – Martha would almost certainly want to honour him with something more than bread and dried fish. He was worthy of a special meal, nothing less than a feast.

Anyone who has cooked a Christmas dinner for a large family will have some empathy for Martha. Some of us may also empathise with the concept of a relative who sits idly by while we are working as hard as possible. I would certainly expect my sister to lend a hand. (Christmas in my house is very much a family affair with everyone helping out in some way.) No wonder then that Martha was unimpressed that Mary chose to sit and listen to Jesus rather than pulling her weight with the household chores.

And so we see that frustration and stress finally get the better of Martha, and she goes to Jesus to protest her sister's laziness and to demand that he command Mary to help.

So what is it about Martha's strengths that have turned to weakness? Why didn't Jesus shower her with praise and do as she asked – deliver a rebuke to her good-for-nothing sister? After all, there was much about her that was praiseworthy. Clearly her dedication to serving practically was excellent. (In John 12 verse 2 Martha is again mentioned as serving dinner. This time it is Lazarus who is reclining at the table with Jesus.) In addition, no one could point a critical finger in her direction regarding her faith. In John 11 verse 27 it is recorded that she declared her opinion of Jesus, saying: 'I believe you are the Christ, the Son of God, who was to come into the world'. And she certainly couldn't be criticised for not conforming with the cultural expectations of her society. As a woman in Biblical times it was expected that she would be the one preparing the meal, whereas Mary was actually engaging in a fairly outrageous breach of etiquette. Women did not sit with the men in such a manner, but here was Jesus giving her his approval rather than giving it to Martha.

Given all of this why was she the one who was rebuked by Jesus? The answer is simple – she had turned her task-related skills into something of an idol. Her attention was so caught up in what she was doing – and doing it well – that she had completely forgotten why she was doing it. Her act of worship had become the be all and end all. You can probably imagine the inner commentary in her mind as she tried to get everything done. Negative thoughts such as: It's not fair. I'm stuck here in the kitchen while Mary is sitting at Jesus' feet. Doesn't he care about me? Why doesn't anyone notice how hard I'm working? Not fair. Not fair. Not fair!

Her biggest strength – serving people well – had become her weakness because she allowed it to isolate her and open the door to negative thoughts about her own worth.

Detail rather than people

Administrators often have to focus on the small details to ensure that things run well. I remember a time when I was entering numbers into an online form – a Companies House annual return - and found the website wouldn't allow progression to the next page until the equations behind the numbers were correctly satisfied. It took several attempts to figure out where things were going wrong but eventually I managed to get the right numbers into the right boxes and I was rewarded with access to the 'Continue' button instead of depressing red wording flashing an unhelpful error message.

Excellence is, of course, worth striving for. It is a value we appreciate at New Life Church in all areas, and it is particularly important for the conferencing business we run. When a client walks through the door we want them to find pristine tablecloths, shining water jugs, and audio-visual equipment that is set up and in good working order. Recently the BBC produced a series that followed the staff at Claridge's Hotel in London. It was fascinating to see the level of detail they attend to in order to deliver their world-famous 'impeccable service'. Being strong on the small detail is not just a helpful asset for administrators, it is a fairly essential trait.

It flips into a weakness, however, if we lose sight of the big picture – the purpose and people behind the activity. When Luke informs us that Martha was 'distracted by (or frantic with) all the preparations that had to be made', the problem lies not with the preparations – everyone needed to eat – but with her focus. She was giving all her attention to serving Jesus, rather than focusing on him as a person.

Imagine if a member of the Claridge's staff team sets out an immaculate red carpet for a guest and then tuts quietly in a corner to themselves when the VIP leaves a dirty footprint on it. The purpose of the immaculate red carpet is to honour the guest, not to remain immaculate.

The danger in church life is that the church office becomes the domain of the administrator and is shaped around them rather than being a welcoming place for others and a centre of service.

Have you ever visited a church and become aware of an abundance of signs telling people to not do this or to not do that? If so, what is probably being communicated is that the administrator is overly focused on detail and needs to readjust to put people first. Of course, it can be extremely frustrating when essential tools such as staplers and scissors constantly vanish. However, the wording on a label can set a collaborative culture rather than a dictatorial one. Which of these two statements would you prefer to find on a label on a stapler for example: 'Do not remove from the office' or 'Please return to the office after use.' The first example is almost accusatory in tone. It implies that the stapler has been removed before and this type of behaviour is not welcome. The second version is much softer and actually gives permission to the person reading it to use the stapler as well as encouraging a community-minded spirit. Small things can have a big impact on the environment.

❑ Are you in danger of putting too much focus on detail instead of purpose?

❐ Take a look at your physical working environment. Does it encourage community and collaboration or does it emphasise rules and regulations?

❐ What steps can you take to remind yourself to put purpose first?

Look at me!

Have you ever seen a professional plate-spinning act at a circus or a variety show? It is fascinating to watch fragile plates wobbling around on tall thin poles. As more and more plates are added to action, we find ourselves caught up in the adrenaline rush of the performer becoming increasingly frantic in their attempts to keep things from crashing to the ground. According to Wikipedia, the Guinness World Record for spinning multiple plates is held by David Spathaky who, assisted by Debbie Woolley, spun 108 plates simultaneously on television in Bangkok, Thailand in 1996.

Administrators often refer to themselves as plate spinners. When I was a full-time administrator I had the phrase in my Twitter bio, and to be honest I think it is still an appropriate descriptor even though my role has changed recently. As administrators we are not only focused on detail, it is generally lots of different kinds of detail at the same time. In a typical day we can find ourselves switching from focusing on spreadsheet-based statistics to assisting a volunteer with a photocopier jam to welcoming someone who has dropped by unexpectedly to handling a phone call from an outside agency. No one told me that being an administrator would involve dealing with a horse that had escaped its paddock and taken up residence on our field, getting to grips with data protection, training staff and volunteers in good safeguarding practices, all while ensuring that we never ran out of toilet rolls and the car park was relatively litter-free on Sunday mornings!

Think again of Martha. As a caterer she would have been very good at multi-tasking, no doubt keeping an eye on her bread dough while boiling water on the fire and chopping tomatoes and peppers for a side dish. As administrators, multi-tasking is part of our DNA. However, the danger with this particular strength lies in the need to guard our hearts. Are we content to be busy plate spinning if no one notices how well we do it or are we secretly motivated by the thought of being at the centre of attention?

How much of Martha's complaint was based on resentment that no one seemed to notice she was working really hard behind the scenes. 'Lord, don't you care that my sister has left me to do all the work by myself?' she cries. Poor Martha – she is feeling very hard done by. As the mother of two boys I lost track of how often I heard the phrase 'It's not fair!' uttered as they were growing up. Reading Martha's story you can almost hear her making the same protest. 'Lord, it's not fair!'

We may love being in the midst of things. We may love putting our skills to good use and juggling all those plates. But we need to watch out that our satisfaction is coming from a job well done, from playing our part in achieving the vision of the church, and not from the warm glow of people's praise and admiration, or even a misplaced sense of self-importance.

Good administrators don't seek to be like David Spathaky, juggling 108 plates on television. Good administration is rarely seen and noticed. If we are not content with that, resentment will soon colour our lives and before we know it we will be muttering 'It's not fair'.

❒ Are you sometimes jealous of those who are in the limelight?

❒ Has the door to resentment opened in your life recently?

The behind-the-scenes prayer

Father God

I thank you for blessing me with the skills of administration, and I thank you for calling me to serve the church in this way.

Forgive me for the times when I have looked for the approval of those around me instead of being satisfied with your approval. Forgive me for the times when resentment has crept into my life and I have allowed myself to believe life is unfair.

Fill me with your love and compassion and your desire to see people released into their gifting. Help me to keep my eyes focused on you, and in all things, to remember I am your beloved child.

Let me hear your voice saying 'well done' and let me be content in that.

Amen

Being too busy to rest in his presence

There can be a real adrenalin rush with being busy. Most administrators are wired in a manner that makes them find delight in the challenge of a lengthy to-do list. Administrators don't tend to be people who long to spend all summer sitting in a hammock in the garden. That's an activity they may enjoy for a couple of hours but sooner or later they are going to be up and about, looking for things to do.

Most administrators are described by others as being 'high-capacity' people. They thrive on busy days. That is one of their strengths. The danger is that being too busy doesn't leave any time for simply resting in the presence of Jesus.

Martha was so busy seeking to serve Jesus and his companions when he came to her house that she missed out on just being in his presence. Even worse, her sister Mary prioritised being with Jesus and was complimented for doing so. Talk about rubbing salt into a wound.

It is important that we don't allow our focus to become so tied into serving Jesus that we miss out on being with him. At New Life Church we ask people to volunteer no more than two Sundays a month. If someone is serving every Sunday it raises a red flag as to why they feel they need to do that.

A few months ago I booked myself a two-day retreat. Life had been particularly busy and I felt the need for some quiet time away. A friend had recommended a retreat centre in the Oxfordshire countryside to me – not too far from home. When I arrived I found it was exactly as she had described – a lovely old house on the edge of a village with views over the countryside. There were sheep in the paddock. A red kite was nesting in the trees and regularly took flight. A stream ran along the boundary of its land. Peace and quiet guaranteed.

I settled into my room, took out my notebook and asked God what he wanted me to do now I was there (note the choice of wording). His response was: just be. Okay, I thought, I can just be with him. After all, how hard is it to 'just be'? After an hour I discovered it was very hard. I was not used to simply sitting in his presence for any length of time.

I went for a walk. It was lovely. The weather was gorgeous. The village was very pretty. I enjoyed walking with him. When I got back to my room I asked him what I should do next. Guess what. He said: just be.

This continued for the whole two days. I had anticipated God speaking to me in a profound way. I was expecting words of direction. But he, very wisely, knew that what I needed was to learn to stop doing, and to simply be. And actually that was more profound than anything else I might have experienced.

When I returned home I felt rested and refreshed in a way I hadn't experienced in all my years as a Christian. I felt loved in a way I hadn't before. And for the first time in my life I had begun to understand what it really means to rest in him, and to be valued for who I am, not what I do.

There is more on this in Chapter 8 *Time out!*, but for now ask yourself these two questions.

❏ When did you last spend time simply being in his presence, not doing things for him?

❏ What steps can you take to prioritise being with him?

The time-out prayer

Father, help me to keep my focus on the purpose of serving, not only on the details. Help me not to lose sight of the people in the midst of what I am doing.

Give me the strength and courage to face up to the truth when I find myself seeking the approval of people for what I do rather than your approval of who I am. Help me to recognise the tipping points where my strengths turn into weaknesses.

And most of all, Father, may I prioritise time in your presence. Help me to rest in you and to recognise that being with you is not only a good thing, it is nourishment for my soul.

Amen

Let it go. Let it go!

In 2013 it was virtually impossible to escape the lyrics of the song *Let it go* from the Disney hit of the year, *Frozen*. If you are a Disney fan, or if you have children of a certain age – particularly daughters – you will no doubt be familiar with the story of Elsa, who struggled to contain her gifting. In a climactic moment midstory she refuses to accept help and shuts herself away. She is the queen of all she surveys, and denying the loneliness of her self-inflicted isolation.

Apologies to everyone who now has the song stuck in their heads for the rest of the day. You are probably wondering what Elsa has to do with being an administrator. The answer is that we sometimes trap ourselves into kingdoms of isolation. And – a somewhat more tenuous link to the song – the only way we can escape is to let go.

One of the strengths of most administrators is their ability to be a jack-of-all-trades. Have you ever taken the time to list the things you can tackle with at a least a fair degree of competency and, more likely, a very good competency? Some of the skills commonly demonstrated include written and oral communications, the ability to use a wide range of software packages and IT equipment, people skills, information skills, a strong attention to detail and the ability to answer any question either from your own extensive knowledge and experience or because you know someone who can fill the gap for you. Chances are too, that in small organisations the administrator is the go-to person for issues relating to human resources (from pay roll to holiday allowances to contract rights), health and safety (first aid in the workplace, for example), GDPR (a recently introduced minefield of administrative red tape to negotiate), and finance (ensuring compliancy with the charity commission's regulations and guidance, not to mention sometimes Companies House too).

Why not take a moment to list your skills?

❐ In what areas of your everyday work would you describe yourself as having a fair degree of competence? List at least five.

It is a good thing to be a jack-of-all-trades. And in small organisations it is almost certainly essential. However, as an organisation grows, more and more expertise and, of course, more and more time resource is required. This is where it can get painful for the jack-of-all-trades administrator because, like Elsa, we may enjoy being the ruler of our kingdom. It can be extremely satisfying to be known as the person who has all the answers, and without whom nothing moves forward. And there is the rub – if we aren't willing to let go of things, we very quickly become the stopper in the bottle neck, preventing growth. Not only that, we will be a barrier to other people playing their part and making full use of their gifting.

Richard, who leads New Life Church, has always encouraged people to hold things lightly, and to not confuse their identity and their value with what they do, rather than who they are. This is often easier said than done.

A few years back we had a team leader who had grown the ministry area that she oversaw really well over a period of three to four years. She was totally dedicated to the role, clearly gifted, and much appreciated. However, after an excellent period of growth, the ministry hit a plateau. After a number of months in which various options were explored to encourage further growth it became painfully obvious that the solution was a new leader with a bigger vision and a larger gifting. Many conversations were held with the current leader, emphasising how much she was valued as a person, but explaining it was time to let go of leadership. She was encouraged to either work alongside a new leader so she could still use her gift in an area she loved, or to explore a different area of ministry and therefore to develop her other gifts. Sadly her response was to leave the church, telling all who would listen that she was unappreciated and had been treated badly.

If we don't hold things lightly we can easily fall into the same trap. Even when we may think we are not clinging onto a role, we can sometimes still run the danger of tripping over a hidden part of an orphan spirit.

When I joined the staff team part of my role was to grow the income from renting out rooms when they weren't being used for church-related activities. It wasn't a favourite part of my job, and it certainly wasn't something I had any experience of doing. In the first couple of years I think learnt a lot of lessons through trial and error, with more emphasis on error than anything else. Despite that, the business did grow. We took on part-time staff to help deliver the service, then a full-time manager who reported to me, and then another full-time staff person and a number of building support staff. We weren't just renting out rooms by this point, we were running a decent-sized conferencing business.

In 2017, I was looking to reshape my role, and God had provided an outstanding candidate to take the business forward. I was thrilled. Clearly his hand was in this. I had even prophesied about a major life change over this person before any of us realised that God was pointing her towards working for the church. Plus I knew I had taken things as far as I could, and if I am honest, as far as I wanted to. I knew too that I had become the stopper in the bottle neck. Handing it over was a cause for celebration.

Why then, did I find myself struggling not to feel that the immediate success of the new manager in the role was in some way a reflection of incompetence on my part?

In my mind I knew that simply wasn't true. I'd done what a jack-of-all-trades does – given it my best shot, grown it as best I could, and then handed it on when it needed someone with more expertise, and frankly, fresh enthusiasm. I was aware, though, that underneath my public cheering of her success was a less than attractive sense of jealousy. My identity wasn't quite as grounded in who I am as a daughter of the King as I'd thought.

There are now at least three other areas that I am consciously holding with a light hand. As we continue to grow, we are in need of an expert in the area of finance who can take on the governance aspects. With an ever-increasing staff team, the human resources work has far-outstripped the time I have available. Health and safety legislation is constantly changing, and we need others to bring their expertise and time. The day of the jack-of-all-trades is coming to an end for me.

The good news is that change can bring freedom. Instead of being fairly good at most things, and stepping in to do things because if we don't then they simply won't get done, a growing team of experts allows for choice. Personally I get enormous satisfaction from anything involving communication – I hope to be involved in that for some time to come. Even there, though, I am aware of the need to develop a team and a future team leader.

❏ Are you the stopper in the bottle neck in some areas?

❏ If so, what steps can you take to let go?

The let-it-go prayer

Father God

I thank you that above all things I am your child, loved by you and precious in your sight.

Help me to remember that at all times, and not to place my identity in job titles and work-related activities.

May I always hold things lightly, being ready to let go and hand on when the time is right.

Forgive me for any time that I have felt jealous of the success of others. Help me, instead, to celebrate the advance of your kingdom in all ways. Remind me that their success is my success because we are one in you.

May I never become the stopper in the bottle.

Amen

Power corrupts and absolute power corrupts absolutely

To close this chapter let's return to the story of Joseph. He is a man who is often extolled as being an excellent example of godly character – some people even say he is second only to Jesus. There are certainly lots of lessons we can learn from him. He remained faithful to God throughout the trials he faced. He demonstrated that he was a man of integrity when he fled from Potiphar's wife. He was clearly a gifted prophet, able to interpret dreams that had an international impact. And, yes, he was a very talented administrator.

However, there is a lesson we can learn from Joseph's life that is not preached with the same frequency and enthusiasm as some of the other stories – the fact that power can corrupt even the most godly unless we guard our hearts. Let's pick up Joseph's story in Genesis 47 verses13 to 25:

> There was no food, however, in the whole region because the famine was severe; both Egypt and Canaan wasted away because of the famine. Joseph collected all the money that was to be found in Egypt and Canaan in payment for the grain they were buying, and he brought it to Pharaoh's palace. When the money of the people of Egypt and Canaan was gone, all Egypt came to Joseph and said, "Give us food. Why should we die before your eyes? Our money is all gone."

> "Then bring your livestock," said Joseph. "I will sell you food in exchange for your livestock, since your money is gone."

> So they brought their livestock to Joseph, and he gave them food in exchange for their horses, their sheep and goats, their cattle and donkeys. And he brought them through that year with food in exchange for all their livestock.

When that year was over, they came to him the following year and said, "We cannot hide from our lord the fact that since our money is gone and our livestock belongs to you, there is nothing left for our lord except our bodies and our land. Why should we perish before your eyes – we and our land as well? Buy us and our land in exchange for food, and we with our land will be in bondage to Pharaoh. Give us seed so that we may live and not die, and that the land may not become desolate."

So Joseph bought all the land in Egypt for Pharaoh. The Egyptians, one and all, sold their fields because the famine was too severe for them. The land became Pharaoh's, and Joseph reduced the people to servitude, from one end of Egypt to the other. However, he did not buy the land of the priests, because they received a regular allotment from Pharaoh and had food enough from the allotment Pharaoh gave them. That is why they did not sell their land.

Joseph said to the people, "Now that I have bought you and your land today for Pharaoh, here is seed for you so you can plant the ground. But when the crop comes in, give a fifth of it to Pharaoh. The other four-fifths you may keep as seed for the fields and as food for yourselves and your households and your children."

"You have saved our lives," they said. "May we find favour in the eyes of our lord; we will be in bondage to Pharaoh."

What we read here is a historical account of the way in which Joseph used the famine to systematically strip the Egyptians first of their wealth, then of their ability to sustain themselves, and finally of their freedom. The earlier steps seem perfectly reasonable: the Egyptians have money and so Joseph allows them to buy food from the stores he had built up over the previous seven years. Note too, that he does not personally benefit from this, rather he passes the wealth onto Pharaoh.

When the Egyptians run out of money he operates a barter system, taking their livestock in exchange for food. To a hungry Egyptian this perhaps didn't seem unreasonable. After all, the only other option would have been to eat their livestock. Exchanging their cattle and sheep for food meant there was always an option to buy them back when things improved.

However, the situation in Egypt continued to get worse. With the livestock of the country now owned by Pharaoh, Joseph ramped up the bartering system by offering to exchange food for land. With no land to call their own the people had no way to make a living. Some theological texts also suggest that Joseph moved the people into the cities, making it difficult for them to reclaim their land at a later date. So, he had very effectively, and somewhat ruthlessly, taken away their freedom, making an entire nation reliant on the benevolence of its ruler, and, as Pharaoh's chief administrator, on himself.

This aspect of Joseph's personality is a fascinating one. On the one hand, it can be argued that he acted in good faith. He kept the Egyptians alive during the severe years of famine, and it appears they were grateful to him.

On the other hand, some scholars point out that when the Israelites were wandering in the desert, God provided food free of charge in the form of daily manna. In Leviticus we read of some of the legal aspects of a society that forbade permanent ownership of land (Leviticus 25 verse 23) because it is to be viewed as a heritage rather than a marketplace commodity. Deuteronomy 15 verse 12 talks of slavery in terms of a six-year time limit, rather different to Joseph's ongoing control of a people who owned no land being required to plant seed and give back one fifth of the harvest to Pharaoh, keeping four fifths to feed themselves and their families.

So what is the relevance of this to us today?

Administrators inevitably wield power – some to a much larger extent than others. As power wielders they can be generous or mean, they can be compassionate or hard-hearted, they can encourage an environment of freedom or they can tie people up in reams of red tape.

Joseph saved the Egyptians from starvation and death. He also used the famine, and his prophetic insight, as a tool to enslave them and to add to the wealth of an already wealthy man. How then should he be judged? More importantly, how will we as administrators be judged in our roles? Will we be heralded as godly people who showed the compassion and love of Father God to all around us? Or will there be an ambiguity in our actions?

☐ Are there areas in your working life that reflect ruthlessness rather than compassion?

☐ Are there areas where you wield power in a manner that enslaves people rather than releases them?

The good steward prayer

Father God

May we be good stewards of all you give us, including power and authority.

May we seek to release freedom and prosperity to all.

Open our eyes to areas where the taint of bondage has crept in and give us the courage and strength to break those chains in our workplace and over the people we serve.

Amen

It's a very subtle thing to talk about strengths and weaknesses because almost always they're the same thing.

(Steve Jobs)

Chapter 7 When it all goes wrong

Most of the important things in the world have been accomplished by people who have kept on trying when there seemed to be no hope at all.

(Dale Carnegie)

This chapter may seem an odd one to include in a book on administration. For a start it contains a very personal story of heartbreak and healing. Why include that in a book about spreadsheets and planning documents? The answer is because we all face difficult times in life and we all live with the paradox of the kingdom being now and not yet. When we go through experiences where the kingdom is very much now – when our prayers, both large and small are answered swiftly – then we can feel strong and it is easy to declare that our trust is in the Lord. However, there are times when the kingdom of heaven can seem very far away and prayers appear to go answered. There are times when we walk through enormous pain and find ourselves questioning everything we have put our trust in – perhaps even questioning the existence of God. This chapter looks at such a time in my life, and is a story of learning to trust God through the times when it all went terribly wrong.

It also contains encouragement to keep going when your world is dark and difficult. Administrators are the people who get things done; they are the vital support crew for the limelight ministries of pastor, prophet, teacher and evangelist. Taking out the support crew is a strategy the enemy can and will use in order to hinder the advance of the Kingdom. And so, when it seems that all is going wrong, it is important that we have counter-strategies that enable us to get back up when we are knocked down. Strategies that enable us to keep going when everything in us is screaming 'Give up'. Strategies that enable us to be all that we are called to be – world changing sons and daughters of the King of Kings.

A time of blessing and busy days

The start of the new church year in 2017 was bringing with it huge blessings, which, of course, also meant a huge workload. For the past 12 months or so we had been preparing people for the changes required to become a multisite church. Sunday 10th September was our last celebration service together in a single venue. The following week saw 150 people meet in south Milton Keynes at a brand new rented venue, and 350 gather in the north at what was now another venue rather than the singular 'home of New Life Church'. It was a huge milestone in the 40-year history of the church, and I felt enormously privileged to be a part of the team that made it happen.

The following week we ran a four-day administration conference from Monday to Thursday with Paul Manwaring of Bethel's iGlobal network, which went extremely well. More than 40 administrators were encouraged, inspired and blessed by Paul's teaching and wisdom. The week after that I was responsible for the logistics for a day-long gathering of over 200 church leaders for Catalyst prayer and fasting, and then I was heading straight into two overseas conferences for which I was providing administration services. And, if that wasn't already a ridiculously busy schedule, I was also still holding the reins for our conferencing business and church-wide operations as the appointment of a new staff member who would take that on had been unavoidably delayed.

I was really tired but determined to keep going, juggling all the balls. But then two things happened that destroyed my equilibrium.

First there was a problem with the venue for one of the overseas conferences. The conference started on Monday and ran through into Thursday, finishing at lunchtime followed by a gathering of about a dozen people for a business meeting in the afternoon. The hotel, however, had taken an exclusive booking from another group for the Thursday, and claimed that they had not been told we needed meeting rooms for that day. They expected us to check out and depart the hotel in line with the checkout times relating to the bedrooms. I pointed out that this was unreasonable, and that exclusivity could not be applied to the hotel's facilities for the whole of Thursday. Most of our delegates had overnight accommodation booked for the Wednesday evening and it is common practice for delegates to still have access to hotel facilities on the day of check out. I quickly discovered that under the exclusivity agreement with the incoming group not only would we not be allowed access to the conference facilities, we would not be allowed to use any restaurants other than for breakfast. Had that been the only issue, stressful though it was, perhaps I could've kept going. But there was worse to come.

Personal loss

For the past nine months, we had been looking forward to the arrival of our first grandchild, and had followed the progress of my daughter-in-law's pregnancy with much joy and anticipation at the prospect of becoming grandparents. By late September she had gone past her due date, but we had no concerns. The pregnancy had gone well and it is not unusual for babies to choose when they come rather than adhering to the dates predicted by the medical profession. However, late on Monday evening at the beginning of October my son sent us a text saying he was at the hospital with his wife. The text was short and incredibly painful. They couldn't find the baby's heartbeat. We were in London at a concert, so we rushed out and headed for the nearest underground station. By the time we reached the platform a second text had arrived. Their unborn daughter – our much anticipated first grandchild – had died in the womb. In the early hours of Tuesday 3rd October Seren Alice was delivered, a beautiful perfect baby who was born asleep in the arms of Jesus.

There is no way to describe the pain of losing a baby. Suddenly all the dreams of sharing a future with them, watching them grow and become all they are called to be, are torn away. Instead there is only anguish. My own grief at losing a grandchild was compounded by my grief for my son and daughter-in-law. Layer upon layer of pain and, dare I say it, the knowledge that I could not fix any of it. As an administrator fixing problems is my reason for being. How could I get through this unfixable experience?

My default when faced with personal trauma has always been to fill my time with activity. When I heard, many years ago, that my father was seriously ill with cancer, I responded by cleaning my kitchen until everything gleamed. I suspect this is not an unusual response. So, for the next week, I attempted to carry on as usual during the week, while spending my evenings supporting my son and daughter-in-law. We cried together. We prayed together. We told each other we would get through this together. Friends and family poured out love and support.

I've always considered myself emotionally strong. I've lost people in the past. Both my parents had passed away. Good friends had died. I knew about grief. I'd done training courses in grief counselling. But this was different. This was raw in a way I had not experienced.

I held it together until, a few days later, I received a perfectly reasonable question about the contract with the hotel, which was in Greece. I knew we didn't have a detailed written contract because we were working with a trusted travel agency based in Turkey, and the culture there is that a person's word is sacrosanct. Email confirmations are generally as close as we get to a written contract. Suddenly I couldn't be the strong administrator who took problems in her stride and always had a Plan B to fall back on, and generally also a Plan C.

I sat on the sofa in my lounge completely engulfed in fearful thoughts. What-ifs of the worst kind – mostly related to work – overwhelmed me. Unable to really process the loss of Seren, I fell into an abyss of negative thoughts, blaming myself for the problem with the hotel – even though it was not my fault – and fearful of what else might go wrong with that event, and the even larger overseas conference that I was administrating at the end of the month. My self-confidence was ripped to shreds. Everything that I had taken pride in – and yes, note the word pride there – suddenly seemed fragile. I no longer believed I was a good administrator. Things had gone wrong on my watch. My trust in God had been deeply shaken on a personal level, and my trust in myself more so.

It is in moments of crisis such as this that we get to see who we truly are. I'd called Richard who, being the great leader and friend that he is, dropped everything and came round to see me. As I sat on my sofa next to my husband I recognised that I had a deep-rooted need to be seen as strong, capable, the one who fixes things, the hardworking trustworthy administrator who always had an answer. I had presented myself as Superwoman, but now the superhero cape was in shreds and underneath it all I was a human being.

The practical needs were quickly dealt with. Richard's diary was miraculously free of appointments, so he took on the responsibility for the conference in Greece. He also swiftly arranged for another administrator to step into my shoes for a couple of weeks regarding the larger conference. The pressure was off. Now all I had to deal with were the many questions that were haunting me. Big questions that I didn't imagine dealing with this far into my Christian life. First, who am I really? Second, how could I trust God going forward when I felt so betrayed? And third, how could I ever find the strength to keep going?

What follows is a brief look at some of the things I have learnt through the darkest days, and some things that may help us to keep going when we really don't feel we have anything to give or any reason to get out of bed. I hope they will be a light in the dark for anyone facing difficult circumstances.

The importance of identity

Before you read any further take a moment to answer this question.

❐ Who are you?

A wise woman from another church recently told a room full of leaders that she regularly asks people this question.

"Do you know how most people respond?" she asked and then swiftly provided the answer.

"Most people respond by telling me what they do. And then they are shocked when I point out that is not the answer to the question. What they do is not who they are."

One of the biggest traps we need to avoid as competent capable administrators is for our identity to become centred on what we do rather than on the fact that we are sons and daughters of the King.

It is a trap that I had believed I had avoided. And yet here I was, staring into an abyss of uncertainty. I found myself questioning everything. My identity as a good administrator was challenged. The problem with the conference might not have been a result of my direct action, but things had gone wrong on my watch. I lay awake at night running through things that I could've done differently – and telling myself I should have done them differently. The devil didn't need to beat me up because I was doing a very good job of beating myself up.

I had to go back to basics and remind myself of who I was – a beloved child of God. I realised that despite my best efforts my identity was still tangled up with what I did, and so I had to repent of that. I had to find my way back to a place where I sought approval and self-worth only from him.

I cannot emphasise too much the importance of knowing our identity in Christ. It is the one thing on which we can stand when everything else crumbles.

Don't be crushed by fallibility

As someone who loves the fictional world of the superhero I also realised that the myth that we have to perfect was in need of debunking in my life. A very simple truth is that it is okay to be both human and fallible. There will be times when we mess things up. Sometimes the error will be very practical in nature. Who has not made the simple mistake of forgetting to include an important attachment to an email? Most of us will just shrug off small errors such as these. But what if we make a mistake with much larger consequences? How do we handle ourselves and others in those situations?

First, let's be courageous and, if we've made a mistake, own up to it. It is okay to be human. We all make mistakes. It is far better to get it out in the open, ask for forgiveness and then focus on rectifying what has happened. A working culture in which mistakes can be brought into the open without fear is healthy. It prevents the enemy getting a foothold and using a situation to distort truth, cause fear, and tempt us into mistrust.

Thomas Edison, the inventor of the lightbulb and numerous other useful objects, famously said, "'I have not failed. I've just found 10,000 ways that won't work." This positive attitude to things not working out the way we hoped or planned provides us with a good foundation for handling problems. When things go wrong, there is nearly always something to learn and to improve upon.

Also, if we have our identity grounded in the right place, mistakes no longer have the ability to be earthquakes that rock our entire world.

☐ Are you losing sleep or feeling anxious about making mistakes?

If so, ask the Holy Spirit to set you free of fear, and make a conscious effort to change the way you think. Adopt Edison's view that a mistake is not a failure. It is a stepping stone to success.

Remember your calling

The first chapter of this book is entitled *You are a gift*, and it focuses on the importance of us knowing our calling. There are few things more important than remembering who you are and what you called to be and do when the world is crashing down around your ears.

Also it is good to remember that there are a number of Bible heroes who went through times of wanting to give up. We've looked at Moses, who was so fed up he petulantly told God he would rather be dead than continue to deal with the Israelites (Numbers 11 verse 14 to 15). In 1 Kings 19 we can also read of Elijah declaring that he has had enough of life, and that facing down Jezebel is all too much for him.

Just as Moses and Elijah were reminded that God was with them, we also need that reminder. And when we are tempted to give up, like Elijah, what we may actually need is some time to rest and restore our energy and resolve.

Never forget – you are a gift and God is with you no matter what your circumstances may suggest.

Trust is a choice

Then there is the whole issue of trusting God in the middle of a storm. I found myself asking a very obvious question regarding the loss of Seren: how could he have allowed this to happen to my family? We had prayed for the baby throughout the pregnancy. We had done everything right. Was this some kind of horrible test he was setting us? If so, how could that be reconciled with the idea that he is a good father who wants good things for his children? Had the omnipotent, omnipresence God, who knew everything about us and was always present, really sat idly by as our granddaughter died? Why, when we prayed for life to return while she was still in the womb, had he not answered our prayers? What was the point of praying for anything if it made no difference?

The valley of the shadow of death had become my dwelling place. But here is a fundamental truth – although we may find ourselves journeying through this valley we are not called to make it our permanent dwelling place.

Little by little over the next few days Father God lifted me out of the very dark place in which I found myself. I remember sitting by the river in my home town one morning and telling him how much it hurt, and how let down I felt. It was a very peaceful place, close to the local Anglican church with its ancient stone walls and bell tower. As I poured out my heart I felt his presence. He asked me to give him the pain, which I did. In exchange I had the strangest impression of him placing something inside me – it is hard to explain other than to describe it as a warm golden glow. Somehow in that moment I knew that he grieved with me. He was not some malicious god inflicting random tests on his children to see how they would react, but rather he was – and is – a good father who was wrapping his arms around me just as I had wrapped my arms around my son and daughter-in-law in the hospital room.

I've always known that trust is a choice. Now I was choosing to trust him in the midst of pain because first and foremost, I am his child. When everything goes wrong in life that has to be the foundation on which we rest. It has to be the core belief because at the end of the day it truly is a key truth. As Paul writes in Romans 8 verses 38 to 39:

> For I am persuaded, that neither death, nor life, nor angels, nor principalities, nor powers, nor things present, nor things to come, nor height, nor depth, nor any other creature, **shall** be able to **separate us from the love of God**, which is in Christ Jesus our Lord.

A mother's journey

Following the loss of our granddaughter we grieved as a family and faced the fear of realising that life is a fragile thing, and that being a Christian does not give us a pass card on the pain of a fallen world. We also realised we had a choice – to go forward or to stay still, locked in a place of grief. What follows is a blog post my daughter-in-law wrote as she came to a place of choosing to move forward.

> Growing up on the coast in the UK, I have a thing for the ocean. At the beach, my Dad taught me that every seventh wave was the biggest. As a child this would excite me as I waited for 'the big one' to overwhelm me.
>
> When we lost our first little girl, Seren, in October, the big waves weren't so much fun anymore. The big waves were the only waves, and now my heart longed for the little ones I could step over.
>
> I had dreamed and hoped for nine long months, only for it to end with the worst sentence I had ever heard: I'm sorry, there's no heartbeat.
>
> I cried until I physically couldn't breathe anymore. I lay in bed for three days and only ate pretzel sticks and thought

about nothing but my girl. I was numb and angry to my core. I demanded that God take away this pain so I didn't have to walk through the darkness that would follow. 'Take it away God. Now!'

But then I remembered the words I had read in a book called *Lean on Me* by Anne Marie Miller. These are her words:

> 'He gently said no as a single wave of his grace washed over me. And then another.

> I realised I had a choice. I could move my heart further from the ocean and let it live untouched and unbothered by this seemingly unproductive task of rebuilding and the fearful task of being vulnerable. Or I could simply sit and let the waters of grace slowly, moment by moment, smooth my heart out. I could persevere.'

The big waves deserved my heart and time because they brought my healing. God is in the waves, in the darkness and he IS the light. While the big waves do not yet excite me, they are welcome as I persevere into the light again; with friends, with family, and with God.

Eighteen months further on, my son and his wife are the joy-filled parents of a baby son, and my husband and I are discovering the delights of being grandparents. Life can be incredibly hard, but God is always good. We can choose to shape our view of God through the lens of our circumstances or we can view our circumstances through the lens of who God truly is.

We can choose trust, and when we do we will discover he is trustworthy.

Get up and make your bed

As you may have gathered by now, I love superhero movies. The first Star Wars movie was released when I was in my teens. I adored Princess Leia. She was smart. She was a leader. She refused to play the role of the damsel in distress. She had a purpose and a destiny and was willing to die to achieve freedom from evil. I so wanted to be Princess Leia.

It can be tempting to try and live up to a fictional ideal in which we are superheroes who save the world. But real life is far removed from a Hollywood movie with its dramatic last minute rescues and big blockbuster set pieces. However, our small everyday actions can change the world of the better and while they may not seem glamorous, they are vital.

In a speech to graduates of the University of Texas in 2014, William McRaven, a retired US Navy admiral said this:

> If you want to change the world, start off by making your bed. If you make your bed every morning, you will have accomplished the first task of the day. It will give you a small sense of pride, and it will encourage you to do another task, and another, and another. By the end of the day, that one task completed will have turned into many tasks completed. Making your bed will also reinforce the fact that little things in life matter. If you can't do the little things right, you'll never be able to do the big things right. If, by chance, you have a miserable day, you will come home to a bed that's made. That you made. And a made bed gives you encouragement that tomorrow will be better.

> (McRaven, 2014)

Think back to Florence Nightingale and her painstakingly recording statistics day in and day out as war raged and soldiers died around her. The heroes of history were everyday people who refused to be deterred from their goals and stubbornly turned up every day to do things that may have seemed trivial and boring. You are a hero today – turning up to make sure the accounts are submitted on time, the paperwork for a meeting is ready, the rotas are emailed out, and there are pens in the stationary cupboard. Don't believe the lie that none of this is important. Celebrate the truth that the small things can and will change the world. Don't give up, no matter what the enemy throws at you.

By the way, Admiral McRaven's entire speech is available on YouTube. If you need a boost on a tough day, track it down and watch it. It will lift your spirits and give you hope.

When we are faced with the darkest of days and feel overwhelmed, let's set our faces against the storm. Let's get up and make our beds.

I wrote this poem shortly after our granddaughter died. I offer it up here as a glimmer of hope for a dark day.

Reboot

The light flickered today, returning to life
A system reboot that had seemed an impossibility
When the blue screen of death kissed our lives.
But there it was, a tiny spark of emotional energy
Looking forward, rather than existing
Day to day, hour by hour in shut-down mode
Numb
Disbelieving
Breathing in and out because lungs demand air
No matter that the heart is encased in stone.
Communicating but not truly living.

It's been two weeks.
Two weeks since you were taken from us
Two weeks since the news broke
Two weeks since our anticipation of the future crashed
And took a different path
Two weeks of stomach-heavy dark grief.
Two weeks of shut down, emergency-mode only.

But today, the light returned.
And with it a choice:
To operate in safe mode or to embrace all of life
Its pain. Its joy. Its shattered dreams. Its future hope.
Reboot.

Punch the shark!

When I had been in the role of church administrator for approximately a month I found myself sitting opposite another administrator at dinner one evening. She had been in the role at her church for a number of years and was keen to take me under her wing and encourage me. However, I was somewhat taken aback when she said that I should call her when I found myself in tears.

"When that happens," she said. "You don't need to sit in your office and cry alone. I am at the other end of the phone. I'll be there for you."

It was a kind offer, and I appreciated the heart behind it. But surely I wouldn't need such support. Why would a job in administration reduce me to tears?

I was also told by other well-meaning people that the average lifespan of a church office manager was four years. Apparently most people have had enough by then and throw in the towel. Now, I have to admit I saw that as a bit of a challenge. I would not be one of those people! When I took on the job it was with the mind-set that I was in it for the long haul. I expected to be around for the next ten years, possibly longer.

What I hadn't taken into account was the fact that like any spiritual role, the enemy is constantly looking for ways to derail administrators. After all, we are the people who turn vision into reality – the ones who make things happen. If he can put obstacles in our way and get us to quit it is like throwing a spanner into a well-oiled machine. Things will break. Progress will stop or slow down.

Here is a further extract from Admiral McRaven's speech to graduates in which he describes a night swim that Navy Seals had to complete in order to pass their training:

Before the swim the instructors joyfully brief the trainees on all the species of sharks that inhabit the waters off San Clemente. [...] you are also taught that if a shark begins to circle your position — stand your ground. Do not swim away. Do not act afraid. And if the shark, hungry for a midnight snack, darts towards you — then summon up all your strength and punch him in the snout, and he will turn and swim away.

There are a lot of sharks in the world. If you hope to complete the swim you will have to deal with them. So, if you want to change the world, don't back down from the sharks.

So be on guard. Expect to face battles. Expect the enemy to play dirty and send sharks after you (or 'flaming arrows' as the Bible states in Ephesians 6 verse 16). But don't give up. Sometimes being a hero is simply refusing to give up.

I have a favourite declaration that has stood the test of time and helped me to battle on. Here it is:

I will not be defeated by fear, stress, discouragement, depression or need because in all these things I am more than a conqueror.

Value community

When I first started to write this chapter, I thought that sharing about Seren would be crux of the story, but I was wrong. There was another journey through the valley of the shadow of death ahead of us.

Early in December 2018, on the day that we expected our eldest son to fly home from Bahrain where he had been serving with the Royal Navy, we instead found two naval officers at our door. They were the bearers of the worst possible news. Our son had not turned up for his flight home, and a search for him had ended when his body was found. His death was accidental and came far too soon.

There is a lot I could write about this experience, but most of that is for another book. The one thing I want to emphasise here is the importance of community in surviving the toughest of times.

As we handled the shock of his passing, and then the early days, weeks and months of his absence, it was the strength of friends and family that carried us through. People arrived at our door with home-cooked meals. Messages of love and support filled our social media channels. His friends created the most amazing book celebrating his life; we will treasure that forever. And with each pain-filled day I wondered how anyone survives such a loss without a community to carry them through.

It is impossible to over-emphasise the importance of community. In the context of administration do find others like you who will be your community. It is important to have people in your life who understand the particular stresses of administrative life – people who will drop you a text or an email to encourage you on the days when the to-do list is full of seemingly impossible tasks. Have people in your life who will laugh with you as you fend off yet another unrealistic request to deliver a 20-page document with a deadline of yesterday. Have people in your life who will step into the breach and keep all the balls in the air while you deal with the personal arrows that the enemy has aimed at you. Have people who greet you with a smile and a hug and who remind you that you are a beloved son or daughter of the King. Have people around you who simply think you are awesome and that you need to be reminded of that on a regular basis.

And be that person for someone else!

The punch the shark prayer

Father God

When it seems like all is going wrong help me to focus on my identity as a child of God. May I never forget who I am in you. May I never forget who you are: a good father who wants good things for me; a father who grieves with me in times of loss; and a father who holds me in his arms safe and secure in good times and in the darkest of storms.

I declare today that I will not allow my circumstances to influence how I see you, but rather I will choose to look at the truth of who you are and allow that to influence my circumstances. I will put my trust in you, even though I may not understand the path that I walk. I acknowledge the truth that when I trust you then the peace that passes all understanding fills my life.

I thank you for your everlasting, totally dependable love. And I declare today that I will set my eyes upon you and never give up. I will walk the path before me knowing you hem me in – in front and behind – and that you walk beside me.

I thank you that you created me to be a gift to the world. And I look forward to the day when I will see you face to face and hear you say:

'Well done, good and faithful servant.'

Amen.

References

Miller, A. M. (2014) *Lean on Me, Finding Intentional, Vulnerable and Consistent Community*, Thomas Nelson (HarperCollins), USA.

McRaven, W. (2014) 'Make your bed', Speech Transcript, Available online at: https://jamesclear.com/great-speeches/make-your-bed-by-admiral-william-h-mcraven (Accessed 19 June 2019). Also available on YouTube at: https://www.youtube.com/watch?v=3sK3wJAxGfs.

Chapter 8 Time out!

To do much clear thinking a person must arrange for regular periods of solitude when they can concentrate and indulge the imagination without distraction.

(Thomas A. Edison

Busy, busy, busy!

Clare gave a frustrated sigh as she reached for her coffee. She had called me a couple of weeks earlier to ask if I knew of anyone who could come alongside her to offer support and mentoring. For the past thirty minutes we had chatted about her role as both the personal assistant to a team of elders and the part-time administrator for a medium-sized church of approximately 160 people – adults, youth and children. As she described her responsibilities I commented that she was actually a PA, an administrator and an operations manager all rolled into one. This was a big challenge that she was valiantly trying to manage on part-time hours. Now, on top of all the day-to-day stuff, the eldership team were asking her to come up with strategies for the future to support church growth. She was keen and willing to step into such a role, but her to-do list was eating up all her time. She simply didn't have any spare capacity.

"I don't have time to think, let alone strategise!" she said wearily.

I suspect most of us who work in administrative roles can empathise. We create to-do lists in whatever format we find works best for us – as I mentioned in Chapter 3 mine is a simple three-column table in a Word document that is easily accessible from the desktop screen of my laptop. And at first, all goes well. The to-do list is a valuable tool that we use to plan and prioritise our days. All too quickly though the tables can turn and, before we know it, we find we are slaves to the list, constantly battling to keep ahead of our – often self-imposed – deadlines.

One of the most valuable things we can do when we find ourselves in this position is to stop and take time out. Yes, you read that correctly. Stop and take time out.

It sounds like madness. How can doing less possibly help us to do more? The simple answer is that it helps us refocus our vision on what is really important, and then to either delegate things we shouldn't be putting time and effort into or to discard tasks that are not actually moving us in the direction we want to head, even though they may be 'good' things to do.

The key to fruitfulness

Recently I noticed a new acronym had appeared in Richard Wightman's diary: TWG. Randomly throughout the week he was blocking out two-hour sessions for this mysterious activity. I was used to seeing entries such as Take Helen to the station – Helen being his wife who works part-time in London. That would shorten to THS and certainly not require two hours of his time. I puzzled over it for a couple of days until the rather obvious explanation occurred to me. TWG stood for 'Time With God'.

Richard has always been good at spending time in God's presence. He is far more disciplined than I am. However, a busy season had caused him to complain that there was never any space in the day to pray and be with the Father. His – very wise – solution was to block out the time in his diary before anything else took up the space.

I was challenged by his determination to prioritise this, but still found myself making excuses that I was far too busy to follow suit. However, I was further challenged by a talk given by a leader from another church that highlighted the fact that prayer and intercession are part of a life devoted to God. This talk emphasised that it is when we stop and spend time in his presence that we become fruitful. Could this be true?

Well, yes. It is a Biblical principle found in the words of Jesus himself. John 15 verses 1 to 5 says this:

> "I am the true vine, and my Father is the gardener. He cuts off every branch in me that bears no fruit, while every branch that does bear fruit he prunes so that it will be even more fruitful. You are already clean because of the word I have spoken to you. Remain in me, as I also remain in you. No branch can bear fruit by itself; it must remain in the vine. Neither can you bear fruit unless you remain in me. I am the vine; you are the branches. If you remain in me and I in you, you will bear much fruit; apart from me you can do nothing."

The outstanding theologian John Piper explores the concept of 'remain in me' in an article on his Desiring God website (Piper, 2018). Rather than 'remain in me' he uses the phrase 'abide in me' which he concludes means this: 'abiding is believing, trusting, savouring, resting, receiving.' So to bear fruit, we need to let go of our belief that it is an outcome of our to-do-list, but rather that fruit is a result of us resting in and savouring the presence of Jesus. It comes through believing and trusting in him. It comes through receiving, not giving. It comes from taking time away from the pressure of the to-do list.

❐ Do you schedule time to stop and simply be with God?

I have to confess I do not find this easy. As I already mentioned in a previous chapter, a while back I booked myself an overnight retreat at a lovely country house in the Oxfordshire countryside.

Two whole days on my own with God, with an expectation that he was going to download some key strategic plans to me as I had recently taken on a new role. And so I sat in my room, relishing the view and the clean country air through the open window. My notebook was at the ready as I anticipated something perhaps slightly less significant than Moses' experience of receiving the Ten Commandments, but nevertheless life-changing. If you've read the chapter you'll know that all God said was 'just be' – for two whole days, that was it.

Once I got over the initial disappointment and, quite frankly, the discomfort of not having tasks to focus on, I can honestly say it was one of the biggest learning experiences of my life. It was also one of the most valuable. I realised that my Christian life was completely focused on what I did for God. To just sit in His presence, to be so aware of him being with me, and yet to not engage in a dialogue about 'stuff' was alien. But little by little over those two days, I found myself doing what John Piper describes as resting in and savouring the presence of Jesus.

I'd lost sight of the fact that prayer and intercession should first and foremost be about an encounter with God. It is about relationship, not about tasks. It is about intimacy with him as well as being about advancing the kingdom.

I wrote this prayer poem after a long afternoon of setting my goals and aims aside, and stepping into the peace and tranquility of simply being with my Father.

Just Be!

My room is drenched in afternoon sun
Golden rays filling the space
With light and warmth,
and the gentle caress of
long dreamy shadows.

What a glorious evening.
What a glorious day.

Father, I declare that today
Brings to an end
The frantic doing of tasks
The stress of too-long to-do lists,
The busy, too-busy lifestyle.
With no time to breathe.

Today I embrace quiet evenings,
long cool shadows,
The whisper of the wind
In the trees.

May I be like the sheep in the field.
Content to graze
Content to wander
To sleep
To rest.
May I be content in you.

Who is in charge of your schedule?

Heading into London for a conference with some staff and volunteers the conversation turned, as it often does, to complaining that life is far too busy. One young woman was bemoaning the fact that she had no time to herself. She works in the medical profession and so has relatively little control over the shift pattern she works. However, what came to light was that she had filled every other waking hour for the next two weeks with either voluntary work meetings or social events. She was feeling overwhelmed by her busy days and evenings. It also became clear that she felt responsible for the well-being of those around. For the purpose of retelling the story let's refer to her as Ellie and the colleague who engaged in the conversation as Rachel.

"If I don't spend time with this person who is going through a rough time, who will?" Ellie protested.

"By all means, spend time them," Rachel replied. 'But on your terms, not theirs.'

Ellie looked bemused as it was suggested that instead of being at the beck and call of the person in need, she should tell them when she was available.

"But …" she began.

"But nothing", Rachel replied firmly. 'You need to take control.'

Ellie sighed heavily. "I know you are right it is just …"

Rachel raised an eyebrow. "Just …"

Ellie sighed again. 'I don't know. Why is it needy people always call me, rather than someone else?'

Now Rachel rolled her eyes and rather bluntly replied, 'The answer to that is simple. It is because they know you are the person who has no boundaries.'

"Ouch!" Ellie pulled a face and considered a moment. "You're right, of course. I don't set boundaries. Oh dear. The problem is me."

Learning to say no!

In Chapter 6 we looked at how our strengths become weaknesses. For Ellie, her compassion for others – a huge strength in her professional life – was a weakness in her personal life because she always put those in need ahead of her own well-being. She simply wasn't very good at saying no to anyone.

Administrators are often in danger of doing something similar and, as a consequence, ending up with diaries crammed full of meetings and projects to the point at which they risk their own personal well-being. Administrators are doers. We fix things. We solve problems. We attend and, quite often, run meetings and projects. And we are often very poor at saying no. No to another meeting. No to another project. No to yet another task on our to-do lists.

❏ How often do you say yes to things, even if it means sacrificing that last hour of free time you had set aside for yourself?

❏ When did you last say no to something?

❏ Can you say no without feling guilty about it?

A couple of years ago I came across a book by Bill Hybels called *Simplify: Ten practices to unclutter your soul*. In chapter two he addresses the problem of not having enough time, and particularly the problem of having a diary or schedule that is so jam-packed with meetings appointments and projects there is no time left for giving the proper priority to vital things like our personal relationships, time with God and nurturing ourselves.

He points out how frequently overly-busy people protest they have no control over their packed diaries, and often truly believe they are unwilling victims rather than recognising they are guilty of saying yes to too much. The hard truth of the matter is that we can control our schedules if we choose to do so. He describes the necessary change as 'grabbing the reins' of our calendars and harnessing its power to serve us instead of rule us.

What is the first step to doing this? Take some time to consider what your calendar would look like if God was in charge of it. How would he have us spend our time each day?

Imagine you are planning your diary for the next month and, wonder of wonders, it is absolutely empty. What would you put into it first? Time with your family? Time with friends? A block of time for your hobby or perhaps time to learn a new skill? Maybe you would put in time for exercise – that swimming session that you keep putting off, time in the gym, or half an hour for a walk at lunchtime.

I have a good friend who puts time for herself in her diary every week. She has a rule that accompanies it – this time can be moved to elsewhere in the week, but it cannot be taken out completely. It is a great approach because it allows her to be flexible without short-changing herself.

As administrators we need to use our skills to protect ourselves in this area. And we need to partner with Father God in decisions about how we should use our time.

Perhaps most important of all, we need to be comfortable with saying no to yet another request for our time and our skills that would eat into the time we have scheduled for ourselves.

Bill Hybels challenges people to create schedules that reflect their most important life goals. The key question we should ask ourselves is not 'What do I want to get done this month?' but

'Who do I want to become in this next season?' Once we know the answer to that we can harness the power of our schedules.

The reason I am sitting at my computer right now writing this book is because I finally reached a point in life where I decided to give some priority to my dream to be a creative writer. (OK, strictly speaking this isn't creative writing because it is a non-fiction book, but a side effect of radically changing my schedule to allow for more creativity was free time to write about this subject – a topic that is very dear to my heart.) Now it is true that I was in the fortunate position of being financially able to reduce from a full-time role to part-time hours (working four days a week), but I was also aware that this was God's timing. A very capable person had come onto the scene who could take on a chunk of my administrative role, and whom God was clearly calling out of secular employment. What did my schedule look like with God in charge of it? Suddenly very different!

☐ Who do you want to become in the next season? Who is God calling you to be?

☐ What changes do you need to make to your schedule to enable that?

☐ Are you willing to grab the reins of your diary and harness its power? How will that change what you say 'yes' to, and how often you say 'no'?

Avoiding short-sightedness

I am very short sighted. I vividly remember sitting in the optician's chair when I was eight years old and being asked to read the letters on the chart on the opposite wall.

"Start at the top and work down as far as you can go", the optician cheerfully instructed.

I peered at the chart, and made the rather reluctant confession that I couldn't read any of it.

I suspect my mother chimed in at that point, probably informing the optician that I had the reading age of a fourteen year old. The problem was not with my ability to recognise the letters on the wall opposite. It was with my eyesight. All I could see was a blur of black on white. I was, and still am, very short-sighted.

Thinking back to those days I wonder how I managed to cope for so long in a world where everything was out of focus. I do remember so-called school friends letting me copy the teacher's blackboard writing from their exercise books because I couldn't read it for myself. There was a price though. I got to copy from their books if I told them the answers to the teacher's questions. I was fortunate to be one of the smartest in the class. But sadly not fortunate enough to avoid my weakness being exploited.

Eventually, though, someone realised what was happening. I visited the optician and was rewarded with a pair of black-rimmed NHS spectacles – no designer options back in those days. The world around me changed dramatically. Suddenly I could see the tops of trees. I could see ships on the horizon when we went to the beach. And most important of all, I could read the blackboard for myself.

As administrators, we sometimes get caught up in short-sightedness because life is busy and we don't lift our eyes from the to-do list to check the horizon.

Do you need to adjust your eyesight today? Do you need to mentally put on a pair of glasses that will allow you to see what is on the horizon instead of what needs to be done in the next hour? Do you need to escape the tyranny of a to-do list that is exploiting your short-sightedness for its own purposes?

An email dropped into my inbox as I was writing this. Was I interested in supporting a funding-raising football match for a charity that we already supported financially as a church? The charity is a relatively small one in the city but it has good relationships with local schools and makes quite a significant impact. My instinct was to say yes, and to add the various tasks involved to my to-do list. To support the event we would need to provide a player for an inter-church football team, and either sponsor that person or assist them in raising sponsorship. It would naturally follow on that we would publicise the event, and I would probably feel obliged to attend personally even though – dare I say it – football bores me rigid.

Fortunately, I'd recently been in a conversation with a group of church leaders in which a story had been told about a budget airline who boiled their identity down to a very simple statement: 'The Low Fare Airline'. Every decision their management team then made was measured against the straightforward parameter of 'Does this action help to make us *the* low fare airline?' If yes, then go ahead and do it. If not, then don't.

New Life Church has a slightly longer vision statement as I discussed earlier. Our aim is to be 'a community that loves God and loves people'. It took us quite a while to settle on this but one thing we liked about it was that it could be interpreted in different ways by people with different talents and gifts. Our pastoral people love people in a very practical way – providing care and support to them. Our evangelists love people by telling them the good news of Jesus and inviting them to encounter the Father's love out on the streets.

So, back to the football match. Would sending a player to help fundraise for a charity that we already support financially help us to be 'a community that loves God and loves people'? Not really. So actually my knee-jerk instinct to add this event to my to-do list because it is 'a good thing to be involved with' was not the right reaction. I needed to lift my eyes to our vision, and not be caught up in a short-sighted response. I needed to say no.

The guilt trap

Do you know the story of the starfish on the beach? Having grown up on the coast this particular modern-day parable is a favourite of mine. It goes like this.

A man was walking along a beach. The sun was shining and it was a beautiful day. Off in the distance he could see a person going back and forth between the surf's edge and the beach. Back and forth this person went. As the man approached, he could see that there were hundreds of starfish stranded on the sand as the result of the natural action of the tide. The other person was throwing starfish back into the water, one at a time.

The man was struck by the apparent futility of the task. There were far too many starfish to rescue. Many of them were sure to perish. As he approached, the person continued the task of picking up starfish one by one and throwing them into the surf.

As he came up to the person he said, "You must be crazy. There are miles of beach covered with hundreds of starfish. You can't possibly make a difference."

The person looked at the man. He then stooped down and pick up one more starfish and threw it back into the ocean. He turned back to the man and said, "It sure made a difference to that one!"

In today's broken society we are surrounded by people in need. Homelessness is a major issue in my city with recent statistics suggesting that as many as one in a hundred do not have permanent accommodation (Slater, 2018). It is shocking to live in a city that, on the surface, appears to economically buoyant and yet has one in three of its children living below the recognised poverty line (Brown, 2019). Loneliness is endemic, not just amongst the elderly, but also amongst those in their 20s and 30s who move here for work and then struggle to find community. Mental health issues are commonplace – people are depressed, young people are self-harming, bullying and harassment is causing teenagers to carry knives for protection. Trust is minimal. Hope is hard to find.

As Christians we know that we are called, like the person rescuing starfish on the beach, to make a difference. Galatians 6 verse 9 encourages to:

> … not become weary in doing good, for at the proper time we will reap a harvest if we do not give up. Therefore, as we have opportunity, let us do good to all people.

How can we then prioritise taking time out when there is such overwhelming need? And when we do take time out how can we avoid feeling guilty about it?

Remember in the story about the busy young woman she asked a heart-rending question:

"If I don't spend time with this person who is going through a rough time, who will?" She was in danger of becoming incapable of helping anyone because she was taking on so much she was becoming a person in need. To find the right balance I believe we need to ask these two questions 'Am I called to help this person at this time? And if yes, then to what extent do I give of myself.' Or to put it another way 'Lord is this person one of my starfish?'

In Acts 11 verses 27 to 30 we read of a prophetic word predicting a severe famine that would spread right across the Roman world. It is interesting to note, though, that the disciples did not feel it was their task to address the whole of the problem. Rather, in verse 29 it is recorded that they decided to help those in Judea 'as each one was able'.

Did they feel guilty about not helping everyone? We can't know the answer to that, but chances are they didn't because they did not take on responsibility for everyone – only those they felt led to help. As in all things, we need to seek God's leading, to listen to and weigh the prophetic, and then to respond 'as we are able'.

Remember too, that when we play our part, God will often step in and do the miraculous. A crowd of 5,000 was fed because a young boy was open-handed with his lunch of bread and fish. Many were blessed with pasta and tuna in the Philippines because I played my – very small part – by being at my desk and answering the telephone. And Acts 4 verses 33 to 35 reminds us of the potential of a group of believers working together in partnership with God:

> And God's grace was so powerfully at work in them all that there were no needy persons among them. For from time to time those who owned land or houses sold them, brought the money from the sales and put it at the apostles' feet, and it was distributed to anyone who had need.

Back in the 1980s I worked with somebody who had become disillusioned about charitable giving. Band-Aid, and then Live Aid, had been a big thing, with pop stars giving of their time and money to fight famine in Africa, and more than £150 million was raised for famine relief. My co-worker was despondent, though. He complained that millions had been raised and yet people were still starving, people were still dying. What was the point he asked?

The point was, I replied, that you and I and many like us made a difference to the lives of individuals who would've starved if we had done nothing. We can't save everyone, but we can save those that God puts in our path. We should not partner with guilt and shame over the things that are not ours to fix. That leads us down a path of feeling hopeless and overwhelmed, and the temptation to believe we are powerless and ineffective. That contradicts God's word that we are more than conquerors (Romans 8 verse 37) and that our prayers are powerful and effective (James 5 verse 16).

It is okay to take time out in order to avoid burn out!

Time to be

Allow the world to rush on by
As you sit and take
the precious time
To simply be.

Deadlines and pressures set
to one side. Live in
this moment, taking the time
To simply be.

Slow it all down, step out
of the race
Let a moment extend
into an hour
And simply be.

References

Brown, P. (2019) One in three children in Milton Keynes are living in poverty, *MK Citizen,* 15 May 2019. Available online at: https://www.miltonkeynes.co.uk/news/people/one-in-three-children-in-milton-keynes-are-living-in-poverty-1-8928433 Accessed 27 July 2019.

Hybels, B. (2015) *Simplify: Ten Practices to Unclutter your Soul,* Hodder and Stoughton.

Piper, J. (20018) https://www.desiringgod.org/interviews/what-does-it-mean-to-abide-in-christ

Slater, R. (2018) 'Workers in Milton Keynes are found sleeping in tents on the street because they are unable to afford local rent', *The Sun,* 7 January 2018. Available online at: https://www.thesun.co.uk/news/5285348/workers-forced-to-sleep-in-tents/ Accessed 27 July 2019.

Epilogue

As the book draws to a close there is one more thing that I wish to share with you. Recently I also came across a writer called Sarah Bessey who posted a thought-provoking article about changing the world on Facebook. It resonated deeply with me as an administrator. I also found it encouraging and inspiring. I hope you will too.

Here is an excerpt from a post, reproduced with her kind permission:

> I used to think that changing the world would be a lot more sexy than it actually turned out to be. I love what Eugene Peterson calls 'the big nouns and the big verbs' – love, justice, peace, shalom, equality, wholeness, mercy, salvation, forgiveness, goodness.
>
> When I was younger and more idealistic, perhaps, all I wanted was to save the world and make things right. Even now, I love that instinct and I still want to participate in that sort of work - it's just that I had this rather wrong idea in my head of how that would look.
>
> Because here's the hand-to-God truth: the most actual *literal* world changing stuff that I get to participate with is almost always decidedly not sexy. It is not public. It is behind the scenes. It is thankless. It is monotonous. It is sometimes disheartening.
>
> And it's the best.

Because it turns out that we only get to those big nouns and the big verbs with all the little nouns and verbs, all the unseen and uncelebrated work:

Like writing letters.
Showing up prepared for meetings.
Writing manuals.
Enacting policy.
Making phone calls.
Voting.
Protesting.
Fundraising.
Having hard conversations face-to-face.
Cleaning bathrooms.
Running for the council seat or the elder board or the strata council or the board of directors.
Making a plan.
Creating budgets.
Filing paperwork.
Feeding people.
Holding the powerful accountable.
Researching the truth.
Training others well.
Writing policy and procedures to protect the vulnerable.
Tithing every single month in one direction.
Consistency of presence.
Listening well.
I could go on....I bet you could, too.

Lots of people love to talk the big game - Lord knows I still love it. We all want the big nouns and big verbs. Yet grand gestures don't actually change the world any more than grand gestures make a sustainable healthy marriage or friendship. People who roll up their sleeves and do the consistent steady good work, day after day, have a better shot of seeing at least a small bit of the justice, the peace, the mercy, the equality for which we are all crying out.

Nowadays my heroes are the ones who have their eye on the Big Nouns and Big Verbs, absolutely, but they are living faithful, steady, never-backing-down, never-sitting-down, hopeful, realistic, never-giving-up, burr-in-the-saddle-of-the-enemy lives.

Paying attention to the details of justice and love and mercy means that it might actually happen for at least one someone. That's why I always say that radical faith is actually just radical faithfulness.

Don't be afraid of getting down in the dirt. Of the hard work. That's where the seeds for those big nouns and big verbs take root. I've found that the Holy Spirit is often most present there in that unsexy daily work of my life than on any stage or any grand gesture. And it's real lasting change.

(Sarah Bessey, 2019)

Acknowledgements

A huge thank you is due to many people who have travelled through life with me over the past ten years. Here are a handful I want to specifically thank within the pages of this book.

Richard Wightman – for trusting in me and always being there for me. Also I thank God for your strategic gifting, your example as a prayer warrior and your determination to keep all of us at New Life Church moving forward in response to God's directing.

Sue Dicks – for listening to me when I've needed to offload, for being a wise and constant friend, for many good lunches, cups of coffee and crazy days of conference administration. You have enriched my life in so many ways.

Rob Davey – for encouraging me to be an administrative prophet, seeking the direction of the Holy Spirit in all things. Your prophetic gifting is a blessing to many, and I thank you for the many times you've gently encouraged me.

Liz Green – for dreaming up the title of this book, and for always being a positive and joyful influence when our paths cross.

Paul Manwaring – for teaching me that administration is a gift of the Holy Spirit and to appreciate its value both for myself and in others.

Nigel Ring – for being an inspiration long before I ever imagined serving as an administrator.

Sarah Malcolm – for always having my back with prayer and prophetic encouragement.

Maria Cowie – for proofreading this book and offering encouragement and insightful comments along the way. Also, for being an absolute rock for us during the most difficult of times – you were and still are a God-given gift to us.

Other books by Sharon J. Clark

Seats in the rain: Poetry for contemplative moments.
Available as a paperback and for Kindle on Amazon.

About UCAN

Since 2009, UCAN (UK Church Administrators Network) has led the effort to support church administrators across the UK and to promote the Spiritual gift of administration within the church.

We are a relational membership network of administrative practitioners who believe that the local church is the hope of the world and that effective administration is crucial to maximizing the church's impact.

Find out more about UCAN at **churchadministrators.net**